# Starting Up On Your Own

**FT** Prentice Hall
FINANCIAL TIMES

In an increasingly competitive world, we believe it's quality of thinking that gives you the edge – an idea that opens new doors, a technique that solves a problem, or an insight that simply makes sense of it all. The more you know, the smarter and faster you can go.

That's why we work with the best minds in business management and finance to bring cutting-edge thinking and best learning practice to a global market.

Under a range of leading imprints, including *Financial Times Prentice Hall*, we create world-class print publications and electronic products bringing our readers knowledge, skills and understanding, which can be applied, whether studying or at work.

To find out more about Pearson Education publications, or tell us about the books you'd like to find, you can visit us at **www.pearsoned.co.uk**

# Starting Up On Your Own

How to succeed as an
independent consultant
or freelance

Pembroke Branch Tel. 6689575

*Mike Johnson*

**Financial Times
Prentice Hall
is an imprint of**

Harlow, England • London • New York • Boston • San Francisco • Toronto • Sydney • Singapore • Hong Kong
Tokyo • Seoul • Taipei • New Delhi • Cape Town • Madrid • Mexico City • Amsterdam • Munich • Paris • Milan

**PEARSON EDUCATION LIMITED**

Edinburgh Gate
Harlow CM20 2JE
Tel: +44 (0)1279 623623
Fax: +44 (0)1279 431059
Website: www.pearsoned.co.uk

First published in Great Britain in 2008
**Retitled edition published 2009**

© Pearson Education Limited 2008, 2009

The right of Mike Johnson to be identified as author of this work has been asserted by him in accordance with the Copyright, Designs and Patents Act 1988.

ISBN: 978-0-273-73117-7

*British Library Cataloguing-in-Publication Data*
A catalogue record for this book is available from the British Library

*Library of Congress Cataloging-in-Publication Data*
A catalog record for this book is available from the Library of Congress

10 9 8 7 6 5 4 3 2 1
13 12 11 10 09

Typeset in 9.5/13pt in Din Regular by 30
Printed by Ashford Colour Press, Gosport

The publisher's policy is to use paper manufactured from sustainable forests.

# Contents

## 8   Developing the business  133

*To my son Cameron, in the hope that this book may inspire him to one day join the ranks of the free.*

# Acknowledgements

As always there are lots of people who 'influence' a book. I suppose in this case it is the hundreds – probably thousands – of independents I have met over the years. However, I would like to thank some of the 'usual suspects' whom I always seem to ask for their opinion: this must mean I think they are pretty smart! To save them arguing about who has had the most influence on me, I have placed them in alphabetical order.

**Rai Barbour**: a towering artistic talent, who carved a second great independent career in his seventies + **Cliff Dennett**: for showing me how the new generation is going to do it + **Mike Devlin**: for thousands of ideas – trust your sell-out to 'big' business doesn't last too long + **Hanneke Frese**: for all your help, and welcome to the 'real' world after those years in the 'wilderness' + **Labeed Hamid**: for 30 years of free advice, and I still need it + **Neil Irons**: the very epitome of the lone consultant, and his staff think so too! + **Shay McConnon**: consultant *extraordinaire*, magician and friend. Pulls rabbits out of hats for cabaret audiences and his clients + **Richard Savage**: a corporate suit turned good guy, who regularly helps the needy – ME! + **Susan Stucky**: a shrewd West Coast observer of the profession, who has forgotten more than I will ever learn + **Nick Winkfield**: a much used, abused and appreciated 'shoulder to cry on', usually after bottle number two!

Very special thanks to my accountant **Peter Clegg** of Westlake Clark for agreeing to be my 'expert' on the numbers, rules and regulations.

Also, huge thanks to **Stephen Partridge**, who first had the idea and whose persistence got this version published. Finally, to my old friend **John Humble**, doyen of the independent consultants, who first suggested that I 'escape' corporate life and go out and do 'something useful'. That was in 1982 and I am still trying.

Mike Johnson

# Foreword

Chances are, if you have picked up this book you are thinking, at the very least, about the idea of taking that big step and GOING IT ALONE. Well you've come to the right place. This book is about getting you ready to be a successful independent consultant and, once you get operational, how to develop your business and stay the course.

The concept of this book is simple. It is a practical, how-to guide to becoming a working professional consultant. All the other books on this subject I have looked at seem not to be books at all, but lists of things to do. Well, there are lists of things to do in here as well, but I think the most helpful parts are the anecdotes about what I – and others – have experienced in running our own small firms; the upsides, downsides and the frankly horrific.

What I have tried to do is give you an idea of some of the challenges you will face and some of the methods and tricks of the trade to deal with them. Essentially, the book breaks down into four major themes:

1 Getting set to go on your own
2 How to survive once you are an independent
3 How to develop the business
4 An in-depth look at the financial and legal implications and obligations

Working for yourself – whatever your specialisation – isn't easy. It takes courage, hard work and, most probably, some luck too. And the harder you work, the luckier you get. More than that it takes enthusiasm and the will to succeed. I started my independent consulting career in 1982 and I have been lucky in the fact that I have enjoyed certainly 90 per cent of that time (I bet few people toiling in the world of big business can say that).

And I use the term 'independent consultant' in its very broadest sense. Whether you are a working mother, a bored employee, a young graduate or even a would-be tree surgeon, this book is aimed directly at you. I don't care what you call yourself, I don't care how you dress or what your expertise is. This book is designed to give you the basics to get going and be a success. In fact, it is really a guide for anyone who is thinking of going it alone – anyone from architects to plumbers, accountants to electricians are welcome.

I hope that you enjoy the book. More than that, I hope it persuades you to join our exciting and fulfilling profession. If you do, may you have as much fun as I've had.

*Mike Johnson*

Little Buckland Farm
Hollywood Lane
Lymington SO41 9HD
United Kingdom
Mikeajohnson@compuserve.com
www.mikeajohnson.com

# Introduction

As I said in the Foreword, if you are not going to go into this with real energy and enthusiasm, don't start. Enthusiasm will get you through most things. If you are just doing it for the money it probably won't work.

There is only one reason for this Introduction, to save you time, money and a load of grief. All I want you to do is quickly work through the short checklist on page 2. If you score under 60, put the book back and go out and seek a different career path.

Be as honest as you can in answering the questions – they are the key to what happens in the following chapters. We get into more detailed questions later in the book, however, this quick test will tell you three critical things about working for yourself:

> ➤ Have I the temperament to do it?
> ➤ Have I the contacts and support that I will need to survive in the short and medium term when most independents fail?
> ➤ Do I have the right skill-sets to be successful in the long term?

If you don't match up to this, there is a very serious risk that you will crash and burn. Countless people try to go it alone and don't make it. They may struggle for a few months or even a few years but in the end one of those three legs of success above collapses under the pressure.

# CHECKLIST 1: HAVE YOU GOT WHAT IT TAKES?[1]

*Score: 1-10*

**Temperament**                                                  *Low = 1, high = 10*

➤ Self-motivated, able to multi-task          _____

➤ Willingness to study and learn             _____

➤ Perseverance                                 _____

➤ Tolerance of uncertainty and risk         _____

**Support**

➤ Good business and professional networks    _____

➤ Reliable personal/family support system      _____

➤ Physical and mental energy                _____

➤ Enough in the bank to 'survive' for six months   _____

**Skills**

➤ Communication skills                     _____

➤ Time management skills                   _____

➤ Transportable professional skills and knowledge   _____

➤ Skills that will not be obsolete in a couple of years   _____

*Total score*       _____

On the basis of your total score, this is what action you should take now.

**Under 60**     *Stay in your job, or find a new one, but don't try to work for yourself just yet*

**60-90**        *Think twice (develop those skill-sets you will need) and take this book with you wherever you go*

**Over 90**     *Do it now!*

Of course, there are lots of other criteria to base a decision on, but the 12 above will give you a quick guide to whether you have the personality, effective support and the required skills to make a go of it. If you scored in excess of 60, then let's move on and begin to outline all the steps you are going to have to take to make sure that you succeed. Not only succeed, but actually have some fun doing it.

We start in Chapter 1, with a very basic, but very important question that most people never ask themselves: WHY DO YOU WANT TO DO IT?

---

[1] Adapted from a concept by Nick Winkfield of Stakeholder Studies, www.stakeholderstudies.com.

# Chapter **1**

# Why do you want to do it?

'*What the hell do you want to work for somebody else for? Work for yourself!*'

**Irving Berlin to George Gershwin**

If you haven't really thought through why you want to become an independent consultant, we can end the book right here. For the simple answer to anyone who hasn't taken the trouble to really examine their reasons in some depth is DON'T DO IT!

In the 20 plus years that I have been working as an independent consultant (or 'independent' for short), I have witnessed all sorts of reasons for wanting to 'hang up your shingle at the door' as the Americans say. To feel that wondrous tingle of freedom, just before that *frisson* of fear shoots down your backbone. And let me tell you, a little fear is a good thing indeed. Or to put it more plainly still, if you can't muster up a goodly helping of paranoia when required, you'll never make it as an independent anything. For independents, paranoia is GOOD. You need it more than enthusiasm, more than brains, more than cunning and the ability to fight. Paranoia is what will drive you in the dark moments. It will stop you from flailing and then failing.

As I have already pointed out in the Introduction, this book is about the practicalities of embarking on life as an independent. Sure you may have a partner, you may have a network, but believe me, you are on your own. Only you, and you alone, can make a success of this foray into a new kind of life – a new kind of business. So, from the outset you need to know, deep down inside, why you want to do this.

None of these are good reasons to go it alone:

> You have a fight with your boss and resolve never to work there again.

> You fail to get a promotion in the organisation and think you can do better on the outside.

> You are made redundant, fired or similar and think it is an easy option to earn some money until another job comes along.

> You go on vacation and decide you want to live in a French/Italian/Spanish/Greek hamlet and raise pigs/wine/olives (please tick as appropriate). Although, joking apart, 'planned' downshifting is a huge trend, which is certainly going to continue (and we talk about that later too).

Avoid the 4D's: discord, disappointment, desperation and daydreams. None of them are good reasons for trying to go it alone. Like all things that are ultimately successful, it takes planning and most of all enthusiasm and commitment to the idea. And don't ever forget that good dose of paranoia just to keep things interesting.

It is all too easy if you are in a job you don't like or feel you are stuck in a professional rut to consider that anything is better than what you have now. It isn't so! As I will continue to stress, you can't live on promises, hopes and dreams. While someone is paying you a wage don't be too quick to throw that away, unless you either have funds in the bank or a contract in your pocket. Why? Because working for yourself is a very dangerous occupation for all of us except the very, very lucky. Know what? I've never, ever met one of those.

# Be a lion tamer, its safer

Depending on what table of statistics you read, working for yourself is a very dangerous occupation that makes test pilots, mercenaries and lion tamers look like sensible people. Why is it so dangerous? Well consider this, two-thirds of test pilots, mercenaries and lion tamers don't fail in the first two years – independents do. This makes anyone's transition to independent status fraught with risk.

And if you go out and question or carry out post-mortems with those that didn't make it (which, while we are handing out advice, is a great idea) you'll find that – swingeing bad luck apart – you can put 90 per cent of that failure down to a complete lack of preparation. Or in some cases a simple naïveté that it was going to be all too easy.

Let's get something straight from the outset, it isn't easy. If it was easy everyone would do it. If it was easy two-thirds wouldn't go down with their ship in the first 730 days. Oh, and that's if you work all the hours, days and weeks that God sends. If you take weekends off and play golf Wednesdays, you've only got 468 days to succeed. Sounds like a lot of time but believe me, there's never enough time. What all of us who take this route have to understand is that being an independent is like falling into a black hole. Time ceases to exist as in the real world. Nine to five – pardon? Eight to six? What's that? It isn't about hours, it's about getting your idea designed, fuelled up and launched. You're the test pilot in a craft you designed yourself. When you are at 35,000 feet, you can't say, 'well that's enough for today', can you?

Given the lousy odds against success and the real time commitment you have to put in to have any chance of making it, you can't help but wonder if the people who take this route to an independent career are in any way sane. My view – and this is personal and has no bearing in scientific fact whatever – is that most successful independents are crazy – in a nice way of course. If they weren't, I don't think that many of us could put up with the high and lows, successes and failures that are the typical topography of any independent's existence.

# Star-crossed

And while I hate to bring anything as weird as horoscopes into this, I was once asked early in my independent life what star sign I was. Answering 'Libra', my questioner rolled about laughing. Their view was that any star sign that was signified by high and lows – euphoria followed by doom and gloom (that's why the symbol is a set of scales) – couldn't possibly survive on their own. Their reasoning was that stress and subsequent depression would be the end of me.

So while I may not be much of a fan of reading the stars each morning to see what's in store for me, you may have different ideas. All I can say is, do what works for you. Others have their own ways of dealing with working for themselves: find what works for you and stick with it. Just don't push it onto other people, that's all.

# Independence: the new, new thing

Of course, having said that, we're all human. Therefore, as well-meaning friends and advice givers, we can spend hours – usually in bars or around kitchen tables on rainy Sunday afternoons – debating the pros and cons of putting that great idea into action, or taking your hard-earned knowledge and going it alone.

We can delight in telling our best friends that they are 'insane' (see above), 'totally wrong mentally', 'too lazy', 'too broke', 'too impatient', or just the wrong star sign ever to contemplate going it alone. The more barriers we erect, the more those determined to have a go will knock them down. Come the cold, hard reality of another Monday morning, most of them won't ever take it any further, opting again for that one- or two-hour commute. But increasingly in this early part of the twenty-first century, more and more will.

As became clearly evident in the research for an earlier book,[1] there is a growing feeling – especially amongst working professionals in the 25–40 age group in most countries (Western at least) – that there has got to be something better than the long hours of commuting and working for some large, uncaring, soulless corporation. You can work for MegaCorp for a while – at least until you soak up all the knowledge and training they will give you and you build a stake in society – but after that many of the smart people are thinking something else matters. Going it alone has never been so popular.

[1] Johnson, M., *The New Rules of Engagement*, London: Chartered Institute of Personnel and Development, 2004.

# A trickle becomes a stream

Sadly for the major corporations, the trickle of smart youngish people quitting key roles in their organisations has become a sizeable – and recognisable – stream. Why do I say recognisable? Because these are the smart young people who 10 or 20 years ago would have been the basis for the next generation of top management, the creators of ideas, the generators of the organisation's future wealth. And, no, of course they don't do what the 'Escape to the Country' magazines say and make cheese or keep pigs (well 99 per cent don't). What they do is take their skills and adapt them to a less stressful lifestyle, where life and work can (eventually) be in some kind of balance. And, since they are going to have to work their bums off to make it successful in the short and medium term at least, they are smart enough to realise that they are working in an environment that THEY created, not one forced on them by an employer. Often this makes a key difference. You may have to work hard (when didn't you?), but when it stops, you are in the place you want to be and you are doing something for yourself. And, as the MasterCard adverts say, 'That's priceless'.

This awareness of there being something else and the way to make it happen, isn't confined to the young. Far from it, 50- and 60-year-olds (more often than not with zero debt) are redefining their lifestyles and downshifting, usually in a way that includes some kind of independent work plan. Of those doing this, independent consultants form the huge majority. As we shall see later in the book, technology has allowed all of us to work remotely to an unprecedented degree.[2]

Indeed, major employers in Europe and the US are slowly beginning to realise that such is the drift away from mainstream employment that these wannabe independents are going to be a key component of their employment mix. Despite what you may read in the press, outsourcing isn't confined to India and China by any means; it is equally at home wherever these professional downshifters have chosen to put down roots. And often those roots are not in exotic locales or deep in the countryside. Many – probably most – continue to live in the same town or city; they just redefine what they want to achieve in a different way. The crisis for big corporations is that without these highly trained professionals, they will face long-term talent starvation. And while this isn't the key role of this book, it is important to keep in mind that as more and more people desire to downshift or remake their lives and take the independent consultant option, there will be more and more infrastructure available to support this new career choice. Hopefully someone will make a hugely successful independent career advising stick-in-the-mud, dinosaur corporations that

[2] Estimates by Datamonitor are of 15 million downshifters in Europe.

the talent they need is outside, not inside their organisations. Think of that. What a great idea. Everyone wins. Corporations get to access the best and brightest, when they need them and for no longer than that. Smart, former employees get to live their dreams. Now wouldn't that be a happy ending?

What all this shows is that while there have always been a few independent spirits about, we are really seeing a mass explosion of people lining up to take the plunge into career independence. Indeed, there has never been a better time to do this. As I said earlier, the infrastructure for independent workers has never been so good and neither have the opportunities.

## Have you got a plan?

The first step on the road to an independent future comes at a price. You have to sit down – preferably with someone else you trust to tell you the truth – and really work out what you want to do, how you are going to do it, and where the support to achieve it is going to come from. It is all about assessing yourself – very honestly indeed. Before we get into some of the detail below, here are a few scenarios to get you thinking:

> You are young, single, you have zero savings, you have a great idea, and you want to quit the job you hate to make it work. The hard truth is that unless you have rich parents or relations who believe in you and can give you a no-strings-attached loan, you are going nowhere. No bank is going to lend you the money at anything like a rate you can repay without security. *Advice*: Work hard at that job you have and save a stake to start when you can. *More advice*: If you truly believe that your idea is the very best there is, then working that extra time won't be hard and will enable you to hone your plan to hoped-for perfection.

> **1 TIP** When you have a big enough financial stake to live for 6 months with no other income, that's the time to try. And I did say 6 months. That's the absolute minimum in my view: 12 months is so much better.

> You are living with a partner, you have two children (both at school) and a house loan about the size of the national debt of Albania. You want to start working for yourself. *Advice*: If your employer will give

you a guaranteed contract for, say, two years that will cover your basic outgoings, then consider it. Otherwise wait until someone – or several clients – give you that basic guarantee. You need to be solvent and be able to see an income stream. *Advice*: I don't mean promises of work, I mean a real, signed, legal contract. *More advice*: don't ever let promises go to your head – amazingly, you can't even make soup out of them.

> You are 55 and you and your wife have waved goodbye to the children. You own your house. You've always wanted to open your own boutique consulting firm. *Advice*: Again, try and do a deal with your employer or volunteer for early retirement, with a few days working attached. Downshift your house and release start-up capital if you need to. Ideally, don't go and burn capital, look for an income stream solution.

# Seven, five or three days a week?

Until the twenty-first century came along, independent consultants tended to fall into three distinct categories: (a) the younger professional who wanted to try out his or her own ideas and gain a broader experience; (b) the mature professional who felt he could get more variety acting on his or her own and (c) the super-specialist who was hired for his or her unique expertise. All of these people – again with few exceptions – worked a full working week and often into the weekend. The amount of work they did probably coincided with business cycles and seasons of their clientele. For example, at certain times independent accountants would find themselves working all hours to meet the deadlines for their clients' filing with tax authorities. Others, like management development specialists, would be busy at key points in their clients' year. However, the fact remained that – like actors – if you weren't 'working', you were 'looking for work'.

Today, however, this concept has been firmly hit on the head. What we are now seeing – especially driven by this rash of newcomers to the independence brigade – are many new consultants who have very specific ideas of how long, how hard, where, why and when they will work. So, for example, I know an international tax specialist who works two days a week on average (charging large fees, I should add), but spends four of his other days of the week in competitive sailing. He now charges for both (he runs sailing courses where most of his wealthy customers are his tax clients too). Equally, I have a long-time friend who runs a horseranch in the US (his dream finally realised) but acts as the senior management development executive for his former company. These people are just as much independent consultants as a newly qualified accountant or people development specialist who decides he wants to build his own practice. The only difference is that they are at different stages of their life with different wants, needs and expectations.

## SIMILARITIES COUNT MOST

It isn't the differences that are important, it is the similarities that count in the quest to be a successful independent. Not clear about the similarities? Not too sure how a 4-day-a-week, yacht-racing, international tax adviser is similar to a newly qualified accountant? Well there are three things that make them the same. Successfully the same:

1 They are focused, they know exactly what they want and have gone out to get it.
2 They have a plan and they live with it and for it.
3 They are also flexible and are equipped for change when a new opportunity comes along.

# Consultant, know thyself!

What I am going to show you – and to stress – throughout the course of this book is that successful independents may seem different on the surface. They may be in different professions, from different backgrounds, with different lifestyles and at different stages in their careers, but if you look below the surface, there are a lot more similarities than differences.

My tax consultant friend knows that five or six times each year he'll have to pull a late night or two. Possibly head off to some West Indian island or whatever (where the sailing is equally good) to keep up his reputation, standards and confidence of the clients. But he is organised for that – totally. However, the key to his success is that he knows what he wants and is fully prepared for that. Do not equate success with hours worked or even income earned. Today, for the independent consultant it is not about hours charged or fee income earned. It is about what you have decided works best for you. And that includes knowing when you will have to move just a little out of your own personal 'envelope' to achieve it. Moving out of the envelope is fine, it keeps you keen and challenges you. Moving out of your 'comfort zone' is a different thing entirely. Basically the advice here is, don't do it. Trying out something you are not confident you can pull off is fatal. Simply, one wrong move, a sudden slip and you can quickly ruin your hard-won reputation. Losing client confidence is not an option. So, if you are asked to do something you don't feel qualified to do – don't do it. If money is tight, it may be a huge temptation to try, but I bet you will live to regret it.

2 **TIP** I said don't take on something you feel you can't do, I didn't say turn it down. What you do is find someone who CAN do it, so taking the pressure to find someone off your client. If you're smart you'll make money anyway from a grateful independent colleague – see later for advice on finders' fees.

I have another friend, a hugely successful motivational consultant. For years I was under the assumption that he worked non-stop. Every time I was at a conference, he was there too. Every time I had a meeting with him the phone rang all the time and he was taking 'orders' for his time. It wasn't until I got to know him really well that I discovered he actually works three weeks on and two weeks off. He has done this for the last 10 years and no one else knows – certainly his clients don't. The reason no one else knows is that he never tells them. They call him and say, 'Can you come in on Tuesday next?' The reply goes like this, 'Sorry I'd love to but I'm travelling all week.' He never says, 'well, I'll be on vacation.' So he never really lets them down and they think he is hugely busy, which enhances his reputation and puts him more in demand rather than less. His view is that he is prepared to give up work to meet his lifestyle needs. Now, he wouldn't have done that early in his career, but now he can afford to (in Chapter 3 we tackle the great vacation dilemma and how to overcome it).

3 **TIP** You must set rules for yourself from the outset. It is a diffi-cult discipline to master, but it needs to be done.

As we get into the depths of this book, let us not forget that you do things for the client, but you must set rules for yourself too. Fail to do that and you will never be successful. There are times when you just have to say 'No, I can't do that right now.' And then you have to understand the hardest truth of all. No matter what you have done for them, how good you are, they may well not come back. They'll find someone else. So you have to become like my friend and be travelling next week. Get them used to that. Play by your rules not theirs as much as you can. The other option is to have someone you can trust who can fill in for you. Again, this is something we will visit in detail later in the book, but beware if you need to do this. Make sure that it is YOU who is in control of the situation. My rule (at least until you know someone very well indeed) is never to pass an acquaintance over to a client. For example, have you any idea how hungry they really are? In my own experience, hungry people can do strange things.

Now I will concede that saying 'no' can be really difficult if you are about to embark on a solo career. I will also concede that you may well run yourself ragged in those early years to get a foot on the ladder of success. And in doing all that, understand why you are doing it. For YOURSELF, not for THEM!

Sure, you can run yourself ragged, but, in so doing, the thing you need to ask yourself is, 'Will any of my clients really respect me?' In my experience, they won't. You may have given them all your time for weeks and weekends, but if they are up against it, you are just one independent. You are – in truth – at the very bottom of the food chain. Therefore, there are two things you need to hold on to in any client relationship:

1 your self-respect
2 your control over the relationship.

Certainly, there will be times when you doubt yourself and doubt your own wisdom/sanity/ability to continue. However, if you know you have done the best you can, then you can take real comfort in that.

But in doing that, a great deal of that comfort can be drawn from setting the limits and rules yourself. How you deal with and react to a client in the early days sets the pattern for your future relationship. But if you want to be happy, not to mention successful and valued, the words are 'Consultant, know thyself' and what you will and will not do.

This applies to all of us. Of course, there is a tendency to look at the outstanding consultants who have made it. But those are not the people this book is for. It is about the basics that will get newly minted, solo workers up and running, whether you are an accountant looking to change your lifestyle, a working mother who wants to work from home instead of facing the daily commute, or even an employee who has negotiated a work-from-home deal. All of those people need a plan, a reason to get up in the morning and go to work – even if it is (temporarily) the kitchen table.

My whole independent career has been about having a plan and sticking to it. Getting up in the morning and knowing what I want to do that day. Yes, I am the first to admit that it doesn't always work out quite the way you planned, but if you don't have that plan, you have nothing. If you are going to be a successful independent, you have to know where you are going and why – and be prepared to evolve as conditions in the market change.

The ones that fail in this business are the ones that don't have any clear plans or goals. I know – or should I say knew – too many consultants who came to consulting on the back of a big pay-out package from their former employer. What they did was 'play' at consulting; they never 'got' it. One built a horse-stable in Kent and spent all their time there, occasionally calling me up moaning that there wasn't any business out there. Well there was, he just wasn't looking for it in any kind of planned way. And without the plan – whatever that plan is – it just won't happen. If they had agreed with themselves, 'Well I want to work three days a week, now what do I have to do to make that work?', they would have been organised. Galloping around a field with a mobile phone in your belt isn't prospecting for work. Neither is rubbing down a horse while making prospect calls. Amateurs are amateurs because they do it for fun and they won't succeed.

> **4** **TIP** Consulting isn't fun – it's business. Don't get that and you don't get fed: it's that simple. But get it right and then it's fun too.

Another person I know well had a similar experience. She was 'encouraged' to leave the cosseted confines of the corporation where she had been for 20 plus years. She never realised how to get into the right frame of mind to be a consultant. She expected work to arrive in her lap. It doesn't: it's hard work getting work. She never found ways to be able to translate her great talents inside a big business into a valued external adviser. The upshot of this was that after a miserable 24 months or so, she got herself re-hired. When we meet we just don't talk about it. No plan, no enthusiasm and, sad to say, no talent for the role. Before you leap out of a cosy corporate corner, consider long and hard whether it's the right move for you. And I mean that in the strongest possible terms. There are a huge number of extremely talented, high-earning employees in the marketplace who are very, very good at what they do. They assume – wrongly – that working for themselves will be easy. For some it is – it's natural. For others, even the very brightest, it can be real living, working hell.

It doesn't matter if your plan is to work one, two, three or even seven days a week as long as you know it and you know how to plan for it. That is what being independent is all about. As long as you know what you're doing, you've got a real chance of making it. As long as you make sure that the one day a week you've decided you want to work (lucky you!) is for that assignment, task, whatever, that's fine. It's playing at being a consultant that doesn't work – ever for anyone, anywhere, anytime.

And that obviously includes how much you want to earn. There is absolutely nothing wrong with saying 'I only want to earn X', if that is what satisfies you. Independent consultants are not like those corporate road warriors of the big firms, trying to maximise every hour. Many of us do our 'jobs' for a variety of reasons, so it's not just about making money. Most professionals I know – the ones incidentally who are the most successful – are doing what they do because they like it (or love it). The money is nice too, but secondary. Sure you need the basics of the bottom line to be in place, but most solo operators do it because they want to or because it affords them the right kind of lifestyle (which is more than simple monetary reward).

One other point to consider. We've talked about enthusiasm and motivation – you need them both big-time. Of course, a lot of energy helps too. As your own boss you could choose to lie in bed every day. If you do, you probably won't make it. You see, most independents are passionate about what they do. Early mornings and late nights don't faze them.

> **5** **TIP** If it's just about money, then think again. All the successful consultants I know enjoy their work, profit comes second.

Now let's look at some of the real issues that any aspiring independent consultant would do well to consider long and hard before taking the leap into what (at best) is an alternative lifestyle. You can make it what you want, but it IS alternative. It isn't 9 to 5, it is the way you need to structure it to make it a success.

# Chapter **2**

## Are you an entrepreneur?

*'Belief in magic did not disappear when our ancestors stopped painting themselves blue. The more difficult the problems we face the more we yearn for the outsider with the magic wand. Corporate leaders have come to rely on the latter-day counterpart of the magician: the consultant.'*

**John J. Tarrant**, *Drucker, the Man who Invented the Corporate Society*

# Could this be you?

Do you think of yourself as an entrepreneur? Do you dream of your photo on the cover of *Fortune* or *Business Week*? Are you a closet Bill Gates or Richard Branson? You are? Well, too bad for you: you'll never make an independent consultant. You see, entrepreneurs want to live a dream – a big dream. They want to create an empire for themselves by building a business and getting lots and lots of other people to help them do it. The independent wants exactly the opposite. They want to stay small and stay – for the most part – in the background. Success for the independent is a job well done that the client usually takes the credit for!

That's where the buzz for the solo consultant comes: telling small, medium and large companies that ought to know better, how to do it. Thinking around that, I imagine the world's most successful independent consultant ever was the late Peter Drucker, adviser to many of the most successful and powerful corporate chieftains. He always worked alone, never had an office and if you called him you usually got his wife Doris.

Drucker didn't know it – perhaps he was too occupied changing the corporate world – but he is the model of the successful independent consultant of the twenty-first century. Front, as in fancy office, has been replaced today by an office in the garden or the attic, the secretary by a bank of electronic gismos and your partner or children. It is a more relaxed – and in fact more productive – environment. One of my great friends, who was consulting from Belgium to some of the world's greatest corporations, used to scare new callers to his home when his sons conspired to put 'unusual' messages on his answerphone, usually accompanied by ghastly, ghostly music or the latest heavy metal hit. Such was his competence that no one ever complained (well, at least, not directly to him).

So the successful consultant isn't really an entrepreneur in the true sense of the word. Of course, they need to know how to sell, but they don't need that 'stack 'em high and sell 'em cheap' sort of mentality. Independent consultants are just that, solo operators hired for a competence that is either unique and therefore valuable, or in short supply in their client's business. (For those who need to know quickly, how to sell comes in Chapter 5).

# The multi-tasking megastar

If not an entrepreneur, the solo professional needs one big talent that breaks into a lot of pieces. They need the ability to:

> work for and please three, four or more clients at the same time (the term multi-tasking doesn't begin to cover it)

> be CEO, CMO, CFO, R&D director, CIO and then the rest at a moment's notice.

In my 25 years of doing this stuff, I have not met many consultants who do all this very well. Most of us get by in a lot of areas and then are very good at, hopefully, the key things. Those key things amount to the talents and skills and experience that you, personally, are offering on the marketplace. It may be your local town, a region, a nation, Europe, the world. It doesn't matter, it is the intrinsic things that you bring to the party that you'd better be good at. All the other stuff you can – if you're really crap at it – get someone else to do, at a price, of course. Please, please, please if you are enthusiastic about something, but not very good at it – don't try, you'll fail.

While there's a lot more about how to do the tasks that independents have to face later in the book, knowing how to 'budget' your time to get the best results takes practice and a certain amount of trial and error to get it right. If you ever get it completely right for longer than a fortnight, please let me know, I'd love to hear how you did it!

Consider this. When you have client 'A' shouting down the phone ('they wanted it in Chicago yesterday, but we only just got the data'), while you are finishing off an urgent ('if we get this wrong we'll all get fired') report for client 'B', knowing that you haven't begun the proposal to client 'C' and your accountant wants your quarterly files for the VAT return (and you had promised to get that promotional e-mail out and meet with your IT expert), don't whine. Get on with it! Believe me, it's better than the alternative of waiting for the phone to ring, e-mail to pop up or fax (who has one these days anyway?) to appear while rubbing down your horse in the stable.

> **1** **TIP** If you can't sell and can't ask for the order – you'll starve. Simple as that. There really is no other solution.

You can look at it another way. If you are really bad at something in the long shopping list of needs to be a successful solo player, farm it out to someone who's good at it. Of course, you'll have to pay for it, but it may be the best solution. My belief is this: get the basics right (the things that bring in the bottom line bounty) and then buy the rest at the best price you can afford. However, in start-up mode do try to do it all yourself. You don't want extraneous costs outside of good accounting and legal advice.

What you cannot do though is get someone to replace you. Because YOU – in the great scheme of things – are all you've got. If you lack motivation, find it difficult to work on your own, hate meeting people, can't communicate and can't 'ask for the order', you won't get very far. While there may be courses that can give you some help, or boost that sagging confidence, most independents have these skills in natural abundance, and know how to use them. If you are the kind of person who has been 'fed' work for their entire work career and has never had to present or create a proposal, you may well need to think again or put it off until you have gained experience. (The other alternative is to work in a large consulting firm where your limitations in certain areas may never be noticed.) None of us – and I mean NONE of us – can be good at everything. For example, I hate to make 'cold calls' even if I have what I consider a good reason. On the other hand, I'll go and knock on anyone's door, happy to meet face-to-face (this is probably lucky for me as I may have ended up as a telesales consultant instead).

So each of us has hang-ups, phobias and things we are plain not good at. What we need is a score sheet which when added up, gives us more than a two-thirds chance of succeeding (go back to the 'Have you got what it takes?' questionnaire on page 2 in the Introduction if you must). A large part – I can't stress this too much – of giving yourself that chance is whether or not you are able to build an effective, dynamic network that can help drive your business forward from day one.

## How's your network?

Chances are, if you are headed for a life in the solo lane, you've been attending a lot of networking events. Well good for you! Only one problem. In my experience, the people who attend network events are people like you, looking to cut loose and set up in business on their own. Go to most of these events and what you'll end up with is a pocket full of business cards with titles on them like managing director, managing partner and senior associate. All of them are one-, two- and three-man bands. Networking events are where people go to lie to each other about how well they are doing and posture a bit, trying to look as prosperous as possible. It's a sort of C-list celebrity outing. Think about it: if everything they tell you was true, they wouldn't be there but sunning themselves on an atoll somewhere in the Caribbean. I was once at a chamber of commerce event in a certain city (taken as a guest) and I was the only person there who wasn't a recruitment consultant!

So when I ask the question, 'How's your network?', I mean YOURS. The personal one built up and lovingly maintained like a classic car over many years. That is the network and if you don't have one like that, you are fooling yourself that you are ready to fly (see 'How not to fall at the first hurdle' on page 33).

Your network is your key, your lifeline, your father confessor. If you don't have a real one, then give up. Because it cannot be manufactured or bought, It is the result of many years of careful nurturing. You can't buy one, or suddenly invent one. A network is something that develops over time.

> **2  TIP** If you are not a natural networker, admit it. Look at your contact file and ask yourself honestly, what can it do for you?

Too many would-be independent operators also make the mistake of believing that the network equals sales opportunities. Wrong, very wrong. While your experiences might be different, I may use my network to help me find opportunities, but they rarely give me any direct business. But the power of endorsement is what you need. It goes something like this: 'You need to talk to Mike about that, he's done a lot of work in that area.' That's what networks are for, that sort of professional referral that money can't buy. And if you have to pay a little homage in the form of a percentage of the fees to the person who did you the good deed, well, who cares?

As you begin to get into the idea of going it alone, realise that you have more than one network. You don't think so? Oh yes you have. There's a central one that possibly has fewer than a dozen really close people. After that are another 20, 30 or 40 good contacts. Beyond that another hundred plus, possibly even thousands. It is made up of everyone who has ever given you a business card and you therefore 'own' their e-mail address and probably their mobile number too.

Good networks, depending on what you plan to do in this independent world, start with the basics: mum, dad, sister, brother, old school pals, even sad, old uncle Charlie. Because, whether you like it or not, they are close and they know stuff. They know stuff about you (some of which you don't want told, of course), but they are often the most honest and the most supportive. Networks need to know stuff, that's what they are for. It is absolutely no use being able to say, 'I have this huge network of people I know' if they can't help you or don't really know who you are. If you call members of your network people you bumped into in the dying hours of a professional conference or at a trade show, then think again – they just don't count. In the need-to-be-honest stakes, have a real look at your 'network'. Just who are they and what will they ever do for you? Remember, the word here is honest.

If you are going to succeed as an independent, you need a network that lives, breathes and can do things or get things for you. If you are really any good at it, you will have begun it years ago and it will have happened easily – because you are a natural-born networker. You were a junior solicitor, accountant, art director, personnel executive and when Fred and Frieda left, you stayed in touch. When Bill left for the big break at MegaCorp, you stayed in touch. When you moved departments or jobs, you stayed in touch.

Ten years later, you have the network to die for. Its tentacles have spread. Now your network is made up of people not just earmarked for the top, but practically there already. They are in Hong Kong, New York, Paris, Brussels. That little acorn has grown, and now it is you who have a strong, sturdy tree, where every leaf is a valuable contact.

Your lap-top, palmtop or Rolodex becomes your bible. In times of trouble, it is a comfort to know it is there. Always up-to-date (oh yeah!) and ready to come to the rescue. Networks are dynamic, they change and evolve, but if they are to work, you must devise ways to keep them current and stay in touch.

3 **TIP** Going to a network event is not networking, that's just looking at other sad souls who don't have a real network. Real networkers, of course, are too busy to be there.

Other people's networks are your networks too. Need an introduction to the XYZ company: who can help you? If you have a real network you can use their network. Why are networks great? Well, if you have just 50 people you can call on the phone and say 'hi' to, and they all have just 50 people, that's already a network of 2,500 people. That should keep most of us out of trouble for a while.

So a quick word of advice here. If you are planning to go solo, sit down and list your primary and secondary networks and then throw in the rest. Then honestly ask yourself 'What can these people do for me?' If the answer is 'nothing', be charitable and keep sending them a New Year's card (well you never know, they elected George Bush didn't they?). But if they look promising, call them. Yes pick up the phone. They don't need another bloody e-mail in their lives do they? Find reasons (there's a lot more on this in Chapter 6) to talk. Keep that real network valid and up to date. For myself it has been a lifeline that I attend to assiduously.

## WELL DONE AUNTIE

When I wrote that piece about Uncle Charlie is part of your network, several readers of the original manuscript laughed. It wasn't meant to be funny though. One of my best friends got the biggest break of his solo career from his Aunt Margaret. He told her what he was about to do and she just happened to have a regular golf partner whose husband was the chairman of a major construction company. A week later he had an assignment that took him around the world. Ten years on, he still does it. Got him started, still paying dividends. So go on, say hello to Uncle Charlie, buy him a drink, ask who he knows.

A friend of mine tended his network garden from the comfort of a senior corporate financial position, maintaining a card file in his home study. When he took, or was 'helped' to, early retirement, he invited all his major customers to a farewell party (the company he was 'retiring' from paid for it too) and he picked up three assignments to act as an internal financial policeman – he's still doing it.

You don't get that sort of deal talking to like-minded people at a network club. What you want are people with completely different minds, jobs, problems and issues. Or, preferably, people with very little in their minds at all. What we all need to keep at the forefront of our activity is that the independent consultant has to pray each day that organisations will continue to do what they have since the Industrial Revolution, i.e.make big mistakes. If they really knew how to manage, they wouldn't need you.

Finally, there is the other part of your network – the part you give business to. Thinking of going it alone? Well you had better get to know where you will find the best accountant, best IT adviser, best solicitor, best IT support and so on. As you create your office (we will come to office set-ups and planning in Chapter 9) you will need these people, so get to know them before you need them. It pays off big-time. Just think, your electricity supply goes out: your IT infrastructure collapses. Do you know the electrician, the IT expert? You know, the one who will put you to the top of his call list so you can get up and working within an hour? If you don't, you need to. Today's world runs on technology – or it doesn't run at all.

## THE OLD BOY'S CLUB

The greatest networks are the ones that you can't buy your way into. They are comprised of the former employees of some of the world's major corporations. The concept is that employees have reunions, or as they move from country to country they join the local 'club'. Some are actually sponsored by the ex-employee's firm (believing that it helps business). If you are into one of these, it can be a goldmine. Being part of one of these is an opportunity to meet a successful group of former colleagues in a relaxed atmosphere. Does business get done? Of course it does. I have a long-time head-hunter pal who built his entire business on the back of belonging to three of these. Three! that's a licence to print money – possibly forever.

Network, network, network is a mantra that needs repeating. I estimate that I add a name a day, and probably remove one too. I just had a stretch break and realised that I have 743 people on my e-mail list, of which a good 300 I can call for one thing or another. So let's use my earlier equation on that. If everyone that I feel comfortable calling (that 300) have the same number of 'live' contacts as I do, then my secondary network becomes 90,000. A lot of business comes down to mathematics in the end. Having access to 90,000, rather than 9,000 or 900 seriously ups the odds on survival. And that is what you want before you bet on yourself – an inside track to success.

A final piece of advice on this network thing. Even if you have a job in an organisation with no specific plans to go it alone, real networking is vital. Too many people call me up and say, 'I just got fired, do you know any headhunters?' These are people who never ever call you back while they have jobs, because they are too busy. What I tell them is, the time to get to know a headhunter is when you HAVE a job, not when it's too late. So even if you picked up this book at your son-in-law's office, take heed. Real networks are not just for would-be independents, they are for everyone – even those people with real jobs.

There is one other item. You can, once established, consider setting up your own network. I did it and it is very rewarding. For how to do it, see Chapter 7.

# What about money?

When taking the plunge into solo swimming, the part of the plan that takes on the most crucial aspects is the financial one. While we will deal in detail with the financial implications of being a solo consultant in Chapter 11 (where my own accountant Peter Clegg takes a long hard look at what you need to consider and we also have a website devoted to keep critical details up to date), there are some basic points that belong here.

I don't know anyone who has succeeded in any professional activity as an independent who didn't have a guaranteed cash-flow before they began. And the word to stare at here is 'guaranteed'. Promises are no good at all – as I have already stressed, you can't eat them.

The upside, for most of us working as independents is that the actual cost of getting started is relatively low. If you are doing it on the cheap, a phone line, broadband, lap-top, phone, desk and some simple office supplies will get you started (various options and scenarios are given in Chapter 9). But, that aside, don't try to simply wing it and hope some money comes in. Save up, or get an iron-clad contract that delivers money into the bank on dates agreed. You can spend your redundancy cash (half of it would be more sensible) if you really must, but I wouldn't recommend it unless you can see a definite return on your investment fairly quickly.

As far as borrowing is concerned, my view – we are not manic, success-driven entrepreneurs remember – is that you don't need a loan, you can get going with very little initially if you are careful about budgeting. The secret of effective and successful independent operation is to keep those expenses (your outgoings) as flat as you can, for as long as you can. Certainly there will be times when it makes sense to spend, but you need to be pretty certain it will pay off 75 per cent of the time.

For all of you who have worked for any type of company, I am sure you will have experienced the day when, although everything is going well and the order book is full, the CEO orders a cost-cutting exercise. Why do they do that? Simple. Every business – and this applies to an independent too – gets soft. So it pays, every couple of years or so, to look at those outgoings and see what they are. Do they provide value, could you buy them cheaper, do you need them at all?

Ultimately, there is no difference between you the one-man-band and ExxonMobil, except they have more zeros after the numbers. Big companies stay in business because they are smart and know when to sign on at the corporate equivalent of WeightWatchers. We should do the same.

If slashing expenses from time to time is a cathartic process, maintaining cash-flow is, I consider, vital. This is the very life-blood of any business, large or small. To use my own example. When I started I had a contract that paid monthly with my former employer for two years. What I did (I cannot believe how sensible I was!) was to live off the money from that contract and bank anything else I made. The result was that at the end of the two years I had a healthy bank balance (leased Mercedes here I come). It also meant that if or when I got into trouble, or clients were late paying, I could fund myself and my suppliers, because I had the cash to do it with.

While start-up costs for an independent can be kept to a minimum, you have to take into account all sort of 'contingencies' that may arise. 'Opportunity costs', having to travel at your own expense in the hope of landing a piece of business; the possibility of having to delay delivery due to a sudden (even non serious) illness like flu; or a client paying you later than planned. All these can hit hard at the cash-flow. So money in the bank (yours, not theirs) not only brings peace of mind, it helps you operate to the maximum of your capacity.

A final tip. If cash-flow is important, then of equal importance is invoicing. If you don't bill, you don't get paid. I have known many independents in start-up mode, who get so swept up in the execution and excitement of work that they forget to send out invoices (few solo workers actually enjoy preparing fee and expense invoices). Being tardy with your invoicing can do more to ruin cash-flow than anything else. Also remember, companies – especially the large ones it seems – are taking longer and longer to pay. I find 120 days can often be the norm. So, you have to budget to cover the payment patterns of your clients. Of course, you can complain. Unfortunately in my own experience, the David and Goliath scenario doesn't play out quite the same way. Taking on big companies – unless you have a very good inside track – just doesn't work too well.

# Home Alone: creating your workspace

Do you remember the movie *Home Alone* and how a young kid got accidentally left behind by his parents in the family home over Christmas? Well, when you throw away the security blanket of job, work colleagues and the rest, you'll know just how he felt – lonely. Hopefully, you'll also be able to take your revenge as he did, and the last scene will be a long and happy one.

But taking that big step is daunting. Because for the first time you are moving out of the known world: YOUR known world. Interestingly enough, no one seems to be able to explain why some people succeed and others don't. Psychologists will tell you all sorts of things about people who are self-starters, brimful of self-confidence and so forth. They may be, but that isn't the secret. Others will talk of people with great technical skills that will always be in demand. But if no one knows where you are and how to contact you, that won't work either. Equally, the old adage of 'build a better mousetrap and the world will beat a path to your door' doesn't really work unless there are a lot of signs pointing to where the door is. Of course, self-belief goes a long, long way, but without some sort of workspace it won't take you very far.

So the first thing that anyone contemplating the life of an independent consultant needs to consider is just how and where are they going to work. While we are going to address these issues in more detail in Chapter 9, anyone contemplating working as an independent needs to start out with a clear idea of how they are going to set up the workplace environment. While this may differ depending on your actual professional needs, there are some basics that remain constant. And if we are going to fully examine the possibility – or better still ability – of someone to go it alone, the right kind of physical space is a major concern.

For example, can you really work from home? Not just for a week or two, but all the time? If you have a partner and children, that may prove difficult unless you can create a 'no go' area where you can work undisturbed. And, as an independent's life can be unpredictable, it needs to be a place that can be accessed 24 hours a day.

And by undisturbed I mean no distractions at all. I know an independent psychologist working from home who has a room (specially soundproofed), with a dedicated, totally private external entrance, so that she can carry out confidential discussions with her clients and they can arrive unobserved. No one is allowed in that room under any circumstances at any time. A freelance film director I know has his studio in his house. He has five children and none of them has ever been in his 'office', even though there are many weird and wonderful gadgets to be discovered there.

## DEDICATED RULES

It is all about setting rules for yourself and sticking to them. I work from a home office across the driveway from my house. My young son has 'visiting time' when he comes in from school. And at weekends we explore together at Daddy's desk. But when I am in full work mode on a project, he knows that it is not a place for him. When I wrote my last book, the dedication on the inside flap read, 'To my son Cameron who resisted visits to Daddy's Office, except for bringing the six o'clock *verre du vin*.'

Once those rules are established and stuck to, it makes life a lot easier for everyone. Think about it. If you were going to work in a business you wouldn't take the wife and kids with you would you? Well it is the same here. As we will examine later, how you set yourself up in terms of physical space often depends on circumstances, location and budget (especially in the early years). But setting rules and sticking to them rigidly from the outset can make up for a lack of physical space.

## DRESS FOR SUCCESS

It doesn't matter how weird or bizarre it might seem to others, do what makes you the most comfortable. An acquaintance of mine, who set up a thriving personal coaching business from his home, found that he actually missed going to work every day. What he did, much to the amusement of the neighbours, was leave home each morning, stroll down to the bus stop and back, and begin work. For the record, he also dressed in a suit and tie every day as it made him feel 'more business-like'.

The advice to take from this is, if it works for you, do it. And a word of warning. It is all too easy for most home-working independents to become pretty sloppy about their dress. I have to confess that I have sinned as much as the next person and have to have a 'talk with myself' every so often to make myself look respectable enough not to shock the Fedex driver!

Incidentally, few people whose lives are based around the Monday to Friday commute have any idea at all about what goes on at home during the so-called work hours. To their initial alarm, the novice home-alone independent quickly discovers that distractions can come in a variety of shapes, sizes and disguises. Newly 'free' home workers report that until they tried to get some work done they had no idea what went on in their neighbourhood. Mail delivery, special delivery, couriers, catalogues, passing sales people, market researchers, gardeners and a hundred and one other distractions all make a bee-line for the home worker. For others, noisy neighbours and their children are a curb to their hoped-for productivity. One of my friends reports that her neighbour still doesn't understand that she works from home and calls her for a coffee most days to make her feel better until she gets a new job! So rules are paramount if you are to get anything done.

Then again the opposite can apply too. There are those of us who can find working alone – especially if they have little need to travel – very limiting and socially excluding. No one to share your coffee break with. No one to go to lunch with. No one to share ideas with. In these cases, it is a good idea to consider some sort of office-sharing arrangement. With so many people becoming independents these days, even the smallest town seems to have some dedicated office space to suit the solo operator. Often these have shared services (like photocopying, bookkeeping, IT support) and can provide the necessary 'buzz' and collegial atmosphere that many people need to get the most from the working environment.

## The perils of partnership

Of course, not everyone feels comfortable working on their own – even in a shared office arrangement. Many need a work colleague to share their hopes and fears, ideas and opportunities. While deciding to work with someone else – or a group of people – can seem like a great idea, care needs to be taken before you commit too much. Time is not only a great healer but a great destroyer of relationships (especially work-related). While we will examine the legal aspects of creating partnerships and companies and the like in Chapter 11, a few basic words of advice first.

Over the years I have seen dozens of partnerships fall apart which, on the surface at least, seemed like a sound concept. In most cases, it is not usually the case that familiarity breeds contempt; rather, the reasons for creating the partnership, and the personalities involved, change over time. For some obscure reason we imagine that partnerships and other legally constituted working relationships (companies, networks) continue forever without needing to be changed or evolved. The irony is that many of us earn our living by helping companies to grow and develop, while at the same time our own business just continues along with the same tired, inappropriate model. Should we be surprised then when things fall apart?

Experience tells me that very few partnerships will stand the test of time. Nothing, it would seem, is forever. Many are put together as an 'escape plan' from another consulting firm or a way of exiting a company. Others are the formation of like-minded (at the time) people. All I would say is think hard and make sure that the legal and financial processes are all in place to guard your future. The happiest independents I know are those that work alone. They may have loose alliances, they may have great networks, they may have business colleagues who pass them business (and they may well give it out too), but they keep 100 per cent control of their own destiny. And what this does is allow you to make your own choices about where to take the business next: your own way, in your own sweet time. Let me give you three examples to illustrate what I mean.

# Independents are really loners

First, because there is nothing like your own experience, let me say out-right that I have been there myself. Yes, I took on a partner. I had a business that at one time employed in one way or another upwards of 15 people. However, it was my business, I owned it 100 per cent. At a certain point I wanted to diversify my own activities – not least in writing books – so wanted to have someone to help run the operation. It seemed to me only right to give them a stake (in this case one-third) of the business.

Although this person, who became the junior partner, had worked with me for some years, working as an employee is very different from being a partner – even a junior one. Basically our ideas of the business differed. Simply put, we were at different stages of our lives and I wanted to move on to other challenges. The outcome was that we parted company. The longer-term outcome is that I would never, ever do it again. In hindsight I realised the mistake: that after 15 years of running my own show, I should have kept it that way. Independent consultants are just that – independent. All the good ones are autocratic and just want to get on with what they do best. They may employ people, but they run the show the way they want to, that is possibly what makes them successful.

# Changing people, changing times

Some years ago, I met a group of five young professionals. Enthusiastic, full of energy, of a similar age and background, they were all working for a large consulting firm. Over lunches, dinners and late night drinks they hatched the great plan that countless groups before and after them have done: 'Let's go and work together, let's be independent'. They did. They were a success – for about three years. Then something happened, which they didn't notice: the dynamics that had brought them together and made them succeed had slowly and subtly changed. When the five began their 'group independent' existence, they were all single, practically all of one mind. Three years later one was married with children; one had been married and divorced; another had inherited a large amount of money; another had married into a lot of money; and the fifth had developed a golf mania. It was like a bright star that had shone for a while and then exploded into pieces, scattering the talent.

Five years after the group broke apart, two of them are successful again as independent consultants. We talk about it sometimes and they realise that any partnership – whether it be with two, three or more people

– will always change. Fail to move it along or accommodate the needs of all the partners and you destroy the reasons for having it in the first place. And even if you stayed aware of the changes, would that be sufficient? Probably not. Nothing like this lasts forever.

## Adding expertise

A good friend of mine had a wonderful business as a motivational consultant. Highly successful and always in demand, there was one downside. Everything came back to him. He had tried to train others to do what he did, but it never seemed to work, the clients always wanted him personally. But what he wanted was to stop travelling five and six days a week. He wanted to stay at home but his clients wanted to see him. One day he had a great idea. 'If I put everything I know onto a password-protected website and sold it, I could earn money while I sleep.'

My friend went out and looked for partners. He found two. One was an independent sales consultant, the other – predictably – an IT expert. At first, everything seemed to go well, it was a new experience after all. But as the months passed, I realised that my friend wasn't happy. 'I discovered,' he said, 'that I couldn't work with these people. They didn't understand the "soul" of my product. I also found out that I couldn't put "ME" into a piece of software.'

The partnership broke up with some acrimony. But there is a very real lesson here. Be careful. Step outside your comfort zone at your own peril. Lose control because you don't know enough and you are very quickly riding on a fast downhill course. My friend is back on the travel trail and has found a better, less stressful solution. He's the guy that takes off two weeks every three that I told you about earlier.

So no matter how good it looks on paper, consider long and hard whether partnership is the right thing to do. I am going to suggest that a full partnership at start-up is 90 per cent doomed from the outset. If you want to go that way, work as independents for a while (pool costs for office space and equipment if that makes sense), but keep your independence until you see how the relationships develop and that takes months, not weeks.

## Bring in the professionals

Most of this chapter has been devoted to the fundamental question, 'Should I do it?' Have I the contacts, the enthusiasm, the attitude, the financial base to make it work? Even if you think you have and your friends think it is a good idea too, my suggestion is that there is another stop to make before you can tick all the boxes – talk to the professionals.

Think about it like this. You are considering becoming an independent consultant, dispensing advice and counsel in exchange for a fee. People come to you because you offer them expertise that they don't have or don't have any desire to develop. Well, before you rush out to buy that brass plaque to screw to the front door, check out your plans, ideas and attitudes with other professionals. If you can get the advice for free, that's great. If not, don't hesitate to pay for it. In most cases it will be worthwhile. What you need before you are 'good to go' are financial, professional and personal assessments.

> **Step 1**: meet with an accountant and explain your plans. Get the detail of what you want to do out into the open. What will it cost to start-up (realistically)? Should you incorporate? What will it cost to run the business? Accountants are said to be boring and dull. Great, they are paid to be that way. Creative accountants are NOT good. What you want is someone who can keep you on the right track – you do the exciting stuff, you pay him to do the boring bits.

> **Step 2**: Talk to some people in the field you are going to work in and in the place you are planning to work. Do you have anything unique to offer? Is the marketplace crowded? What are the fee levels (maximums and minimums)? What's the next 'big' thing?

> **Step 3**: Carry out a personal survey or psychological profile of some sort. These are – I find – frighteningly accurate. You may at first say, 'this isn't me, I'm not like that.' Go on, be honest. Yes you are. If part of the survey suggests that you don't like meeting people and you are not very assertive, go think it over and plan your next move.

**TIP** You are planning to be a professional. So be professional and take the advice of those that know. It is invaluable. Another thing, get into the habit of doing this as you progress in your career. Check out your plans, re-assess yourself, make your accountant (even your bank manager!) your friend and confidant. Often they know more about local business needs and contacts than anyone else in town. They are part of your network, aren't they?

This is really important, because the other thing you need before you can get going is someone (preferably a few people) you can turn to when the going gets tough. And don't think it won't.

# Shoulders to cry on

There was a song entitled, 'When the Going Gets Tough, the Tough Get Going'.[1] Sounds good with a guitar background. Unfortunately it's just another song-writing myth. In the real world, when the going gets tough, we look for a shoulder to cry on – or its equivalent. What everyone – and I do mean everyone – needs are easy-to-reach sources of sympathy. We all make mistakes, unforced errors and are victims of other people's screw-ups too. It is at these times that we need to be able to turn to people who can help out. These are the Samaritans of the solo worker. And, for all sorts of reasons, you need more than one.

Why? Well, sometimes you just need sympathy. Someone who cares about you unconditionally. It could be your old school friend, college chum, drinking buddy, brother, sister or even your mother or father. A person who won't point the finger of blame at you, who won't stir up those, 'it was all my fault' fears. Every independent needs one of those. Hopefully not often, but when you need them, they need to be on hand and easy to reach. E-mails and text messages don't really cut it.

But you also need someone who's been there before you – fought in all the wars, been in all the battles, and who knows the professional issues as well. Someone who is able to offer sound advice and counsel, who has possibly faced the same problems time and again. Maybe he or she knows from bitter experience that they should have done it differently. Now you can learn from that.

When we work for big business, we have work colleagues we can talk to, possibly even sympathetic bosses or supervisors. On your own, you need a replacement set of those work colleagues. The trick about being alone is never to be really alone. Help and succour are just a phone call away. Ideally your professional 'shoulder' will really understand and appreciate your dilemmas, because they have worked in similar environments as you. Probably not doing the same sort of work, but with the same profile of clients. This makes them an ideal sounding board.

I have a great friend who has always been my shoulder to cry on. He always seems to have the right answer. Usually because he has experienced the same thing and knows exactly what to say to me. This relationship is basically one-way, as he never seems to ask my advice

---

[1] *When the Going Gets Tough, the Tough Get Going*: Billy Ocean, 1986.

(probably because I have brought him too many problems over the years); but there are others that are very much two-way. Not only do these people make a very useful cushion for your fears, but they also are the pressure-valve that can relieve tension when you finally resolve the situation and add it to your library of 'war stories'. Most of the time with my 'mates to moan with' we decide, self-righteously, that all clients are bastards and should be strung up from the nearest lamppost. This makes us feel good – well for a time at least.

Of course, there is another thing that you'll need to stay the course as an independent, and that's a nose for trouble. And the bigger the nose, the smaller the troubles you'll get yourself into.

## Can you smell trouble?

I've been fairly lucky in my working life. Most of the clients I have worked for have been major corporations, consulting firms and institutions. Obviously, not all independent consultants are going to have a portfolio of clients like that. If you are working nationally, or within a region of a country, chances are that your business will be based around the local private and public sectors. However, whether you are working for a *Fortune 500* firm or the local town council, knowing that you are going to get paid is critical. Later we'll look at the politics of payment, but for now suffice it to say that you have to rely on your nose to smell out trouble.

Usually following the basic rule of 'turn it down before it turns you over' – is just a matter of how your feel about the project and how the coffers are looking. But, everytime I smelled trouble, it was there. It may have been hidden deep down, but it was trouble. I knew an old advertising professional who used to say, 'You step on a dog turd and you maybe can't see it right away, but it doesn't take long before it starts to smell.' That is sound advice. People who ask for more than they need; people who change the brief; people who are late with the first payment having said that 'money is not the issue here'. All of them are suspect right away. And the one that is the dead give-away is the potential client who says, 'You know, our product is so good that we want to give you a part of the profits. If you work for us, we'll give you a percentage of everything we sell: of course we won't pay you anything until we sell something.' That is how to get poor fast. Also watch out for those who come back to you and try and cut your budget halfway through when you are already committed. Get out FAST. Things will only get worse. That's hard to do, and we've all made a mess of this one at least once in our careers.

There is an old saying, 'If it looks too good to be true, then it probably is.' Hang it over your desk, tattoo it on your arm or whatever. Just don't forget it.

# How not to fall at the first hurdle

I thought that to end this chapter it would be good to list some of the myths of our solitary profession. The reason for doing it here is to act as a warning. Rather like those on cigarette packets, independent consulting should come with a warning notice. It may not kill you, but it can leave you severely battered, bruised, burned and broke, depending on how often you fall down! If you are still determined to make it on your own, read on, we are only just getting started.

Many of these are based on my own experiences, others have been provided by friends and work colleagues. The thing to take from this is, they are all true – tried and tested.

> **WHAT THEY DON'T TELL YOU AT ANY BUSINESS SCHOOL (AND WHY WOULD THEY, AS THEY DON'T KNOW ANYTHING ABOUT IT)**
>
> ➤ All the people (yes ALL) who ever said, 'when you go independent we'll give you lots of work' never, ever do.
>
> ➤ All your 'friends' who you gave work to when you had a 'real' job never answer your calls, e-mails or texts.
>
> ➤ You have ONE chance to set your fees – never lower them, you'll never get them back up again – ever.[2]
>
> ➤ Anyone who asks you to speak for free as it is a 'great network opportunity' is lying. Why would you want to speak to a group of people who are all sitting in front of you earning their salary for being there? Don't let the rest of us down – just say no.
>
> ➤ People do not always cancel meetings even if they say they have. Always confirm before you go and remember you are at the very bottom of their food chain.
>
> ➤ The 'buzz' of feeling wanted is a curse you need to get over. Learn to turn work down.
>
> ➤ Guard your intellectual property with your life! Don't give it to clients. Give them ideas, not the whole encyclopaedia.
>
> ➤ Potential clients can and do steal. Never write a proposal so detailed that they don't need you to implement it.

[2] This is not the same as having a sliding fee tariff. As an independent you can set a range of fees dependent on who you want to work with. Just never let one client know your rates for another.

# CHECKLIST 2: THE GO-IT-ALONE CHECKLIST

My advice is work your way through this and be very, very honest with yourself (if you have got to this point, it looks as though you are getting serious). Also get two or three of your friends to either complete it, assessing how effective they think you would be as an independent operator, or at least discuss it with them before you go any further.

Do you think of yourself as a work-alone, self-starter? Have you any proof that you are?

Do you have any business that you can pick up (guaranteed) immediately?

Will you have to borrow money from a bank or friends and relatives?

Do you really, genuinely, enjoy your chosen profession?

Do you like to play golf/go fishing/go drinking Saturdays and Sundays and will you miss it if you can't do this?

Are you ready to invest in technology to help you and do you know enough about the available hardware and software? Do you have a good supplier/maintenance firm?

Can you be a 'Jack of all Trades' and do things you would not have done as an 'executive' or employed professional that might seem below your previous status?

Can you work long hours without immediate paybacks?

Can you juggle work so that all your clients get the full attention they think they deserve?

Are you able to keep a focus on what you do best and not be distracted from your main goal?

Are you able to be a CEO, strategist, marketer, HR manager, financial director, receptionist and your own PA all rolled into one, every day, 365 days a year?

Can you honestly sell yourself and your services, not once but every day and enjoy doing it?

Can you maximise and extend your network every day? Can you sell every day while you are working on client business? In other words, can you multi-task three, four, five things at once?

Can you ignore the wrong sort of criticism, believing that you are the best?

Can you lose clients, pick yourself up and go and find some more, and keep doing it?

Are you capable of continually evaluating your business and doing what's right for the future, seeing and building on new opportunities?

Do you have good, trustworthy suppliers (lawyers, accountants, IT specialists etc.) who will go the extra mile for you?

Finally, can you smell trouble and have an instinct for bad business deals?

Now, on the basis of your responses, do you really think you should take this idea further?

If the answer is 'yes' then you need to assess your personal circumstances.

# CHECKLIST 3: CHECK YOURSELF OUT

Just how flexible are you? More to the point perhaps, how difficult would it be to make a major change to your lifestyle/workstyle? Without understanding that, it really is impossible to begin to think about starting life as an independent consultant with any hope of lasting success.

1. *What is your current status?*

Are you financially secure enough to launch a career as an independent consultant?

How much of a financial cushion will this provide?

Do you have a pension and can you still pay into it?

Do you have a partner with a job?

Is your partner working in a secure job?

Would your partner help you out with tasks associated with your new work (administration, answering phones etc.)?

Are you convinced that you and your partner are compatible to do this in a work environment?

Do you have children? Are they still living with you?

Do you have elderly dependants to consider now/in the near future?

How important is your community to you (family, friends, local associations etc.)?

Based on your responses, sum up below your present status.

2. *What is your financial situation?*

Do you own your house?

What level of income do you need to maintain your basic lifestyle?

Could you make do with less money?

Can your partner's income provide for basic needs until you get fully established?

Are your children (if any) still at school/college? Do you pay fees?

Do you have elder care and its attendant costs to consider either now or in the near future?

What assets do you have? (pensions, stocks, other savings and holdings)

What of these would you be prepared to sacrifice/put at risk to get the business operational?

What liabilities do you have?

Have you discussed your financial situation with a professional financial adviser?

Based on your responses, write down below your current and likely future financial status.

3. *Just how healthy are you?*

Have you had a medical check in the last 12 months?

Has your partner had a medical check in the last 12 months?

Are you capable of a high (mental) stress job?

Could you put up with a heavy workload, early morning and late nights?

Could you put up with uncertainty about your future success and income?

How would your partner/children feel about this?

Based on your responses, write down below your current health status and how that affects your future plans.

4. *What are the things you really like to do?*

What are the favourite parts of your work/professional life?

What are the favourite areas of your personal life?

Which of these would you be prepared to give up if you had to?

Which of these would you NOT be prepared to give up under any cir-cumstances?

Based on all that, write down below a frank, honest assessment of where you, your partner and your family stand today, and what you would and would not do to get into an independent workstyle.

**Example 1**: 'I am a totally free agent, exceptionally healthy with no close commitments, I would enjoy the challenges of being an independent consultant. I don't mind late nights and unsociable hours of work or considerable travel. Additionally, I have a financial cushion (or a signed contract for guaranteed work) that will cover my outgoings for at least six to 12 months. My pastimes are those that allow me the maximum amount of flexibility and I can give or put aside nearly all of them if I need to.'

**Example 2**: 'Being honest my sense of home and family – as well as the local community – are the most important things to me. I have a partner with a secure but low-paying job that they enjoy, my children are practi-cally through college and I really don't want to go into the stress of trying to survive as an independent at this time.'

..................................................................................................................
..................................................................................................................
..................................................................................................................
..................................................................................................................
..................................................................................................................
..................................................................................................................
..................................................................................................................
..................................................................................................................
..................................................................................................................
..................................................................................................................
..................................................................................................................

# Key learning points

➤ To be a successful entrepreneur you need to be able to multi-task: to be CEO, strategist, marketer, financial director and our own PA all rolled into one, 365 days a year.

➤ You also need to be able to juggle a number of clients/projects simultaneously.

➤ Remember to maintain and keep building your network of contacts. And they may not always be the most obvious ones (remember Auntie!).

➤ Money-wise, keep your outgoings as low as possible, watch your cash-flow and remember to invoice promptly.

➤ Find the right working environment. If that's a home office, make sure you aren't going to be continually disturbed by others in the house. Set ground rules and stick to them.

➤ Consider long and hard before embarking on a partnership. You may be heading in the same direction now, but what about a couple of years down the line? Most partnerships fail to stay the course and most independent consultants tend to be just that – independent.

➤ Before starting up, consult the experts for advice on financial, professional and personal assessments. See if they think you've got what it takes to go solo.

➤ Find a shoulder to cry on (or more than one) for when times get hard. This could be an old school friend, college chum, drinking buddy, brother, mother etc. Preferably though, choose someone who's been there before and fought similar battles.

➤ Rely on your nose to smell out trouble. And get out fast if things turn sour; chalk it up to experience and move on.

# Chapter **3**

# Getting out and getting going

'Don't compromise yourself. You're all you've got.'

**Janis Joplin**

'You've got to take the bitter with the sour.'

**Sam Goldwyn**

Well congratulations! You have decided, even after all the discouragement and seriously scary warnings, to go out and do it – become a true independent. Your days as an employee or a student are numbered. You've checked out all the angles, know who you are, what you want to do and how to get yourself there. But let us remember one big thing before we begin. Now you are committed, the thing you need most of all to get you on your way and sustain you is enthusiasm and self-belief. You have to leave all those nagging little doubts behind and get on with the show. Truth, of course, is that nagging little doubts get exchanged for big ones. The only good reason for not plunging straight in is if you are still trying to make the numbers work in the way you need. Making the decision to get on with the next chapter of your working life even if you have to stick at your job for a few more months is fine, as long as you know you are committed and have a plan to realise that.

While there is no one I have ever met who made the transition to a solo career without some trepidation, they have all had a strong motivation to succeed. But again it has been the planning of the process that has had the biggest impact on their future success. In the previous two chapters we touched on what assets you'll need – both physical and mental – to begin the great adventure. Here in Chapter 3 we are going to look at the transition process itself. What's the best way to start?

To begin, I am going to take some examples of different types of people, all aiming to make an independent career, and use those to take us through the first steps of the transition period. From there, we will get into more of the detail of the daily process and what needs to be in place to make it work. The reason for doing it this way is simple. Today there are so many options and choices that the term independent consultant covers an ever broadening range of people and professional activity. To help as many people as possible make the quantum leap, it is important to put the tasks ahead into the context of your present situation.

## The escaping executive

What executive of any seniority sitting in that traffic jam or crushed in a crowded, standing-room-only train compartment hasn't dreamed of working for themselves at one time or another? After all, they are talented, organised, plugged into their profession. Surely, they think, there must be a better way to make a living than spending almost one day a week stuck in traffic? Well, there is. The only thing you have to consider is, what's the best way to get out?

Many companies today are beginning – albeit slowly – to realise that if they don't make it easier for their talented employees to work in other ways, they will ultimately lose them. So offering long-term contracts, part-time work opportunities and other incentives are increasing in popularity. Most of the choices on offer depend on the age, seniority and expertise of the person about to make that choice to quit.

But there is one overriding common denominator that needs to be kept in mind. Assuming you are not in the firing line, you have value. Like a prize-bull at auction, you have a market price that rises and falls depending on the needs of business. Whether directly or indirectly employed, you can make a contribution to your current – or another – organisation without signing up for life. And this, in fact, is becoming a pleasurable alternative for not only want-to-be independents but the firms they want to leave. Indeed, many firms faced with hiring freezes and departmental reorganisations often welcome the idea to reduce headcount (you) whilst keeping the talent close through a contract to work for a certain number of days each week, month or year. Even the legendary Jack Welsh of GE cut a deal as an independent consultant, although he probably did rather better than most of us in terms of ongoing compensation!

And that is the term that you most need to concentrate on: 'the deal'. If you can get your firm to agree to funding your departure through a contract (even if it is only based on the redundancy compensation you may have got if they had ever chosen to terminate you), you are really ahead. Because they – not you – are funding your start-up operation.

But there are some basic rules to follow to make this happen effectively and professionally. This bit is critical. Don't cut corners, don't act on word-of-mouth promises, pats on the back or friendly handshakes – get everything in writing.

First, carefully sound out the firm and get a feel of what their appetite is likely to be for this sort of get-out-and-go-it-alone initiative. Do they have any formal programme for this? Has anyone else ever tried it and – if they did – what was the outcome? (If possible, don't listen to the answer second hand – try and contact the person who made the great leap.)

Second, know exactly what you want in terms and conditions before you start. There is no point kicking-off the negotiation without being very clear about what you will settle for (possibly try asking for more than you really hope to get as an opening gambit).

Third, make sure you have a way back if negotiations fail. There is no point in cutting yourself off or committing career suicide. Anyway, if you are going to work externally for the firm, you need to maintain their trust and their commitment to you.

Fourth, get a labour lawyer to go over the terms and conditions and conduct the final negotiations or exchange of contracts with the firm. Not only is this more professional, it also takes the personalities and any lingering resentments out of the deal.

> **1** **TIP** Try to get a rolling contract with a renewable clause in there for 6 months before the first term ends. That way if they want to terminate, you'll have 6 months to do something about it.

Finally, exceptional circumstances apart, try and limit the amount of committed time. If you want to develop a business as an independent consultant, you'll need to have elbow room to do that. I would say two to three days a week is ideal.

Of course, if you can't get your firm to fund your venture, the next best thing is to get ad hoc work from them. Again, keep it professional and try and tie them down to some type of long-term commitment, even for a few days a month (the number of days usually creeps up over time). Remember, you know their business, and once on the outside you can show them what a valued asset you can be.

Obviously, some executives and specialists make easier transitions than others. Marketers, communications people, human resource specialists and IT experts often find it easier to set up on their own than financial, sales and production personnel. But there is no real barrier as long as you have a clear plan of what you want to achieve. I know a production engineer who still works from time to time for his old company, 20 years after quitting (he works for their competition too: see Chapter 7 for more on that). Similarly, one of the best salesmen I ever met quit his job (and his excellent annual bonus) and became a freelance consultant. He didn't make as much money but his overall lifestyle improved enormously.

This – of course – is what many of today's would-be independents are looking for: a different way of life and the chance to earn a living as well. Getting out of that daily commute can increase productivity immensely and you will be surprised how much work you can do at home in the time it would have taken you to commute to your old office.

## TURNING A DAILY COMMUTE INTO PROFIT

For the last 25 years I have always worked close to home. First in a second apartment in the same building, then living 'above the business' in a townhouse and latterly in a system-built office across my garden in the country. In every case I was able to put in two hours – at least – every day by not having to commute anywhere. Certainly, you need to go and see people, but when you go back to the office to get things done you are already home. That makes the home-working independent extremely efficient. Something that the average employee (and employer for that matter) rarely appreciate: until they try it themselves! Even a weekend client crisis can be squeezed in between Sunday lunch and walking the dog.

This need to change careers seems to be happening more frequently within the established business community. And it seems to strike young and old, junior, middle and senior management with equal effect. With companies again concerned about the shortage of talent to fund their own ambitions, this should be a good time for those bent on an independent career to score. Companies need experience and labour flexibility, the independent provides that in a cost-effective way that no one else can.

Many who have made the transition from employee to solo worker say that they relish the variety of the work that comes their way. And the things they all say they miss least? Office politics, petty rules and regulations getting in the way of doing the job and the daily commute.

Can anyone do it? Can anyone make the transition from salaried employee to fee-charging independent? Well, if you are going to make it as an independent, you need a large dose of imagination. If you have that, then basically anyone, anywhere can do it. Here's some who have:

> a hard-charging, 30-something corporate lawyer bailed out of her highly paid job to set up a one-woman law firm, specialising in labour law and cross-border hiring:

> a marketing director who successfully transited from his multinational employer to become a one-person, corporate, social responsibility consultant;

> a management development executive in a major retailer became a trainer, coach and mentor to a group of small firms in a rural location, which gave him growing opportunities to do hands-on work.

Then again, others not only switch from employee to independent, they also change their career. Increasingly, in a world full of more and more choice in what we do, people are deciding to turn an interest, a hobby, a passion into an opportunity to make a living. In some locations, younger people are doing it because they feel disenchanted with the kind of life that is imposed on them by the 9 to 5 grind. Recent studies show that up to 90 per cent of 30-somethings feel 'stifled by the rigours and conventions of corporate life'. Worse still – for the employers facing talent famines – reports say that, 'unlike many of their predecessors, these people have the means, the mindset and the technological savvy to do something about it.' Yes, bailing out of the corporate rat-race is becoming more and more common and it is going to increase year on year. But it isn't just the employees of big business who are choosing these other options.

## Consultants bail out too

Working life in a big consulting firm – or even a mid-sized one – isn't any better than that in any industrial or service business. In fact, these past years it has been a lot more precarious. Bonuses may be good in the bumper years, but it can be a hard place to work when things turn sour. Most major consulting firms – whatever their business – have had serious downsizing programmes going on at some time in their recent history. The knock-on effect of that has been a glut of refugees from the big firms choosing – or forced by circumstance – to go it alone. And these are not the ones that failed after the first 24 months either, these are people who are well trained, well qualified and know how to deal with clients. They are – possibly – the best equipped group to go it alone and succeed.

And I am not talking just about management consultants, far from it. They could be accountants, architects, trainers, organisational development experts, consulting engineers, coaches, IT experts. The list is endless.

### DIGGING FOR VICTORY

To illustrate just how diverse opportunities are these days, try this. I met a 30-year-old made redundant from his job in a leading architectural firm, where he had specialised in landscape design. Using his training, he moved to the country with his partner and began a one-on-one design service aimed at assisting private clients to revitalise their gardens. Meanwhile, he sought to retain his consulting status. He employs local builders, fencers, gardeners and tree surgeons to do the manual work, leaving him to concentrate on his design specialism.

And as with employees from companies, consultants can often soften the blow of their departure by getting ad hoc work from their former employer – although the timing can be critical, dependent often on how well their firm is doing that year. Better still, the really smart ones frequently take client business with them! Of course, this is generally frowned upon by employers, so check your employment contract carefully to ensure there is no clause prohibiting such action before you go down this route.

Consultants from large and medium-sized firms who find themselves starting a business offer great services – their training has usually been excellent and they are very up to date with both techniques and technology. So buyers can pick up a highly effective, former big-time business consultant at a relatively bargain price. Also, they have another significant advantage on their side: they know how to sell.

It seems that having been a consultant for a big firm does help open doors. Therefore, if you find yourself in this position and having to sell your services, don't be shy about saying where you used to work – it can be a huge asset to getting your new one-person business off the ground. The only difficulty might be all the others who have also worked for those firms. They make the scene a little too crowded sometimes. Indeed, if all the consultants who claim to have worked for that doyen of the consulting profession McKinsey & Co were to be believed, I have little doubt they would reach to the moon and back!

# Back-to-work spouse meets downshifter

While it used to be assumed that the man of the household would be the bread-winner, today's climate is different. Technology, coupled with the increasingly flexible working options that employers are offering, mean that it is easier than ever for both parents to assume some of the pleasure/burden of childcare. A woman can return to full-time employment and try to negotiate one, two or three days to work at home, effectively taking the drudgery out of the commute. This kind of deal allows a husband to set up a solo consulting firm and still be able to get out and visit clients and prospects. As I said in Chapter 1, all it takes is a plan, a lot of enthusiasm and some imagination.

This kind of approach works excellently for any domestic partnership because it allows one person to work full-time, while the other takes the 'risk' of going it alone. Sensible couples I know work on the basis of living on the guaranteed monthly income for the one still earning a salary and saving the consulting fees to build the business in the future. For many that I have observed, this type of arrangement can have several stages:

> **Stage 1**: Partner A quits a full-time job and, using the income of partner B to live on, begins to establish themselves as a sole trader.

> **Stage 2**: Once partner A has established a relatively steady business model, partner B then quits and using the income from partner A's consulting activity begins life as an independent too.

> **Stage 3**: With both reasonably established, they then combine their talents to create a more dynamic business operation.

However, I have noticed that in many of these so-called 'escape' scenarios, there seems to be a slightly different trend. Please ignore my cynicism:

> **Stage 1**: Partner A quits full-time job and moves to a rural/semi-rural location (insert country here ...............) to start a (insert rural or hospitality-type occupation here..............), while partner B keeps job, lives in tiny apartment in large city and commutes at weekends.

> **Stage 2**: Partner A establishes business and is joined by partner B.

> **Stage 3**: Partners A and B sell business/land/chateau to Megacorp Inc. and move back to bright lights and big city!

Well something along those lines anyway. The point being, that it is YOUR choice what you want to do with your life and people are increasingly plumping for lifestyle first and workstyle second.

As I emphasised strongly in my book *The New Rules of Engagement*,[1] work–life balance is wrong, it is life–work balance that people ascribe to. Everyone has a dream of being in control and the rules and regulations of the modern-day corporation – as I described above – don't suit today's free-wheeling society.

Then again, you don't have to be in a partnership to take the leap into the unknown. Singletons do it too. As do single mothers and those high flyers who just want to spend more time with their children or develop other interests before it is too late. In a society that celebrates – even venerates – choice, we have become a multi-choice world. It's not surprising then that an increasing number of people see being an independent as the way to 'have it all'.

That includes the downshifter. There are a thousand and one reasons why people downshift. Escaping the city, the arrival of children, a personal health scare, death in the family (and getting rich), being made redundant, a sudden inheritance, getting married – the list goes on and on. Again, it is all about having a plan and sticking to it. Determined downshifters are certainly a growing force to be reckoned with. One of my favourites is the jaded management consultant who just can't take the commute and the city life any more. He and his wife (the children had already gone their own ways) moved to a hill village in rural Spain. Three years later, he was the

[1] *The New Rules of Engagement: Life–Work Balance and Employee Commitment*, CIPD, 2004.

business consultant to the local farmer's co-operative, masterminding the branding of their excellent produce all over the world. This is the type of person who, if parachuted into the middle of the Sahara, would find a way to do business (camel psychology?).

# The graduate

Remember the movie *The Graduate*? The famous line from the publicity posters and the book cover, *'This is Benjamin he's a little worried about his future.'*[2] And what does he say to his dad? 'For twenty-one years I have been shuffling back and forth between classrooms and libraries. Now you tell me what the hell it's got me.'

Well Benjamin, you may be the most famous graduate of all time, but you'll be pleased to know you are not alone. Every year more and more graduates shun big business and the rest of the services that support it. Every year an increasing number of graduates take that gap year and never come back. Every year a growing number start their own business. And keeping up those statistics, a large number of them fail. But, for the ones that succeed, they may not think of themselves as 'consultants' in the true sense of the definition, but actually they are.[3] And what they 'consult' in reflects our twenty-first century habits. Like my friend the landscaper (see Box on p. 46), I know of young, recently graduated consultants in fields as varied as yacht design, sports medicine, event organisation and historic building conservation. When you talk to them, it was their inability to get enthused by the 'adult', grey, organised world that determined their future direction. These people are smart, enthusiastic, brimming over with energy, being successful and, most of all, enjoying every minute of it.

For anyone reading this who thinks consultants wear suits and ties and have to have a degree in law or accountancy, forget it. If you've got a great idea and some skills, you can do it too. You will have to work hard at it, but you'll have a lot of fun as well.

Most interesting is that it is often the best and the brightest that are taking this route of school, university, solo employment: fitting into, or simply creating, new independent consulting opportunities. And as I pointed out earlier, this leaves big corporations facing a world of diminishing returns. A decade ago, most of these people would have scrambled to get a job in the company store, happy to have it. Today, they shun that kind of life, because they can. This leaves our big corporations facing a

[2] *The Graduate*, author Charles Webb, 1963: United Artists, director Mike Nichols.
[3] The *Collins Concise Dictionary* defines consultant as: 'a specialist who gives expert advice or information'.

shortage of the exact people they need, the inventive risk-takers that are the real guts of any business. With talent wars and skill shortages impacting most developed countries, this change of direction by the new age best and brightest is significant.

# The early retiree

I suppose you could lump this category in with the Escaping Executives, but in most cases I have come across, the motivations for setting up as a sole trader are a little different. Most have some kind of income stream (pension, investments and so on), so they are not dependent on making a lot of money. Basically, many of them do it because it keeps them occupied and gives them a goal and a role in life. Fifty years ago, their fathers had the garden shed to potter about in; their mothers had the sewing room. Today they are offering their expertise (tied into their former job or their long-practised pastime or possibly passion) for a fee. Not because they need to, but because they want to. Sometimes they do it for no fee at all, because they like it!

I know retirees who – after a long and distinguished career in business or public service – have become some of the best specialist consultants ever. Look at this line-up:

> the managing director of a commercial art studio, whose pastime was Old Masters, is now one of the world's most sought-after fine-art consultants;

> an IT manager, whose hobby was Gothic architecture, is now a consultant to one of Spain's most historic cities;

> the head of human resources of one of Europe's leading corporations, now acts as a consultant in acquiring horses for an Arab prince's stud;

> a former schoolteacher in his 65th year, now teaches conflict negotiation to managers;

> a retired jumbo-jet captain is now the navigational consultant to one of the world's leading manufacturers of sailing craft.

All these people have taken something that was their passion – their 'escape' from the reality of earning a living – and turned it into a job that they enjoy. All of them have told me that if they had known what was going to happen, they would have done it an awful lot earlier. I tell them that if they had tried, they would probably have failed. They are valuable now because it took them years to acquire the knowledge that people are now willing to pay for. Not only that, they are operating well within their comfort zone. They are confident in their abilities, relaxed even. Why? They – unlike many first-time consultants – have nothing left to prove.

But it goes to show that you can be anything you want to be at any age. It also goes to show that almost anyone can be an independent consultant if that's what they really have set their minds on. Now what we need to discover is some of the things you need to do – and some of the things you don't need to do – as you begin to get into start-up mode.

## Key learning points

> Can you get your present employer to 'fund' your transition to independent status by offering guaranteed (or even ad hoc) work?

> If you do a deal, make sure you have a legal document or contract that lays out the terms and conditions in detail.

> Take out the daily commute and work from or close to home, giving yourself 10 to 15 hours a week extra to work on your new business.

> It really helps to have a long-term plan so you have goals to shoot for.

> Almost anyone can be a consultant. Today more and more people are taking the plunge: yacht designers, sports medicine practitioners, events managers and the rest.

> For some – coming up to enforced retirement – independent consulting is the twenty-first-century equivalent of the safety of the potting shed.

# Chapter **4**

# Planning the successful start-up

'Life is what happens while you are making other plans.'

**John Lennon**

'Luck sometimes visits a fool but never sits down with him.'

**German proverb**

# What not to waste time over

If you ignore the rest of the advice in this book – or you're in too much of a hurry to start – read this section below NOW! The reason is, what follows is based on the long – and sometimes bitter – experiences of myself and others like me. We started with enthusiasm, a little common sense (which like a little knowledge can be a dangerous thing in the wrong hands), some capital and not much else. We survived, well not all of us, but we learned as we went along. Now it is my great pleasure to pass on what we learned to you. These are the bits that no one ever tells you, because unless you can get us to confess, we are not going to let you know. Who needs more competition in the marketplace? Well, that's not really true. Most solo operators I know are only too willing to give advice. Sadly, we know that a lot of it goes unheeded. Anyway, I promised the publishers I'd do my best, so here are some of the things you really need to know.

The first thing to realise is that it doesn't matter who you are, what you're planning to do or which country you are living in. Special local business practices and taxes apart, what follows is universal in its application to the independent consultant's operational start-up and on-going work. The areas covered here are in no order of importance for the simple reason that they are all equally important to your survival. Get these right and you are on your way!

# Adminfrustration

This is a word you'll adopt gladly. Unless you are a complete nerd, administration is a pain that occurs somewhere deep in the nether regions. So, if you are not a nerd or a masochist, you need to find ways to deal with it in a quick, painless fashion. First piece of advice is – if at all possible – do administrative work once a week. I know lots of sole traders who do it either very early in the morning or on Sunday evenings. Then you think that it is not impinging on your working. Every business has to deal with administration of one sort or another, there is no way around it. Some have tried, everyone fails. Don't do it and you will lose out – and lose money too.

If you get very busy, or you travel a lot, I would recommend either having a 'helper' who comes in once a week and sorts it all out for you, or using an office services firm. Both are good ways to get these tedious tasks done without costing a lot of money. Most people charge by the hour, which means that if they are not doing anything, they don't bill you.

Years ago even the smallest operator seemed to have a secretary of one sort or another, who answered phones, wrote letters (this was before the PC changed all our lives), booked travel and filed everything. Today, technology has made most of this largely irrelevant. You can do it all for yourself in a fraction of the time it used to take and it all costs less too. But no matter how you try to hide it, the administration just won't go away.

When I started a few years ago to work solo again, my accountant Peter Clegg was honest enough to explain that it was useless having him or one of his highly qualified people do all my administration. He found me a bookkeeper, who came in and did basic tax returns and kept all the paper together (sorting credit card receipts was the bane of my life!). All I do is keep bank statements, travel receipts and so forth in files as they come in. My 'helper', a local freelance bookkeeper, comes in usually once a month and makes sense of it all.

Others use their spouse for this task. Which – assuming they don't mind it and you don't care if they get to see that you spent €300 on a dinner in Rome – can be another way of saving money. Another reason for engaging your spouse in tasks like this is that you can (dependent on national tax laws) pay them to do it, or have them on the board of directors. My company is incorporated in the UK and my wife acts as Company Secretary. This allows her to draw a salary and take dividends. However, it is important to know what the prevailing tax implications are where you operate. Such cosy, keep-it-in-the-family arrangements don't work everywhere and are positively frowned on in others. Currently in the UK, the taxman has a less than congenial view of this type of set-up, but hasn't been able to make too many inroads so far.

The other thing that may well help you is trying to get any of your regular payments on to some sort of direct debit system, so you don't spend time writing out cheques or making payments online. Critical items like telephone and broadband invoices need to be paid on time and if you are out of the office for extended periods, you need to make sure that all this is going to get taken care of automatically. You simply can't afford to get cut off from your client base. Communication is key in this business.

Another tip is to pile up all your payments and do them in one go once a month. That may sound like a very obvious thing to do, but again it takes discipline. I put a date in my agenda and make sure that I take that hour – or whatever it takes – to make payments.

TIP I always make my own payments to suppliers, utilities and other providers. Then I know they have been done and they have been sent out when it suits me, not someone I've hired for the purpose. Keeping an eye on payments ensures that it is YOU managing your own cash-flow. Just seems like good business sense to me.

# Invoicing

It is the same with invoicing. Despite the fact that it is nice to get paid for one's labours, I have never yet met anyone who enjoys the drudgery of raising fee and expense invoices. But if you want to get paid on time, you have to make the effort to get it done. Again, have a regular date for that. Or – if you want to avoid those tardy payers – invoice automatically as soon as you can.

> **2** **TIP** There was a marketing consultant I once shared a project with who got so arrogant that he actually charged to his clients the time it took him to prepare the invoices he was sending them. This is not a good idea, especially when the client finds out, as they did in his case. Something about a breach of trust comes to mind. As they say: 'Don't try this at home!'

Many independent consultants work on a project basis. When I work that way I usually charge one-third up front as the project kicks-off; one-third when (say) the research process is complete; and the final third, plus an accounting of final expenses, at the end of the project. To make sure you don't end up badly out of pocket (and keep that ever critical cash-flow available), I also invoice an up-front expense fee. This is particularly important where a project involves travel, hotels and other subsistence costs or paying your own suppliers who are supporting you. How much do I invoice for an expense advance? Never more than 10 per cent of the total fees, but that could change depending on the business you are in.

The trick in all this is very straightforward. You are NOT a bank. If you don't invoice up-front, the client is using your money. When you consider how long it can take to get paid these days, the sooner you get money in the better. And make sure to add at the bottom of your invoice, 'Terms: strictly 30 days'.[1] Many big corporations pay up to 120 days after your invoice is submitted. Even the good ones may pay on 60 days, which means – in reality – three months after you did the work.[1] The worrying thing about that is most small suppliers (the ones you will use) expect to get paid after 30 days. And if you want to keep your local suppliers happy, you should treat them as best you can and pay them within 30 days. Now do you see why I am obsessive about cash-flow and having money in the bank? And it is all down to one thing – get those invoices out.

---

[1] UK legislation enacted over the past decade allows you to charge interest for late payment. (Late Payment of Commercial Debts [Interest] Act 1998, amended and supplemented by the Late Payment of Commercial Debt Regulations 2002.) If no credit period has been agreed, then the Act sets a default period of 30 days after which interest may be charged.

# ... and the X-Files

The other part of Adminfrustration that all sane people hate is filing stuff. But unfortunately, that is a necessary evil too. Again, the best thing is have a tray, box, drawer or whatever and pile it up and do it all at one time. Either put a date in the agenda (as above) or save it for a wet day or when a client or prospective client cancels a meeting. Personally, I don't recommend getting help to do this. If you are a true independent, you need to know where the material is filed and you create a system that works for you. Casual office help and freelance bookkeepers rarely stay for more than a year or two. If the taxman comes calling five years down the line, you need to know where things are, otherwise they'll just take up vast amounts of your time that you could have avoided.

## LOST IN TRANSLATION

During my work life in Brussels I had a French-speaking secretary who joined full of enthusiasm and fresh from secretarial college. I left on a two-week assignment and she decided that in order to learn the business, she would take my rather sad filing system and completely re-do it. 'Great', I thought, 'what an excellent idea.' On my return, I went into the office on a Saturday morning when no one else was there and needed to consult some files. I couldn't find them anywhere and eventually gave up. When my new secretary appeared for work on the Monday morning I asked where was the file on printers and the one on general suppliers. 'Under 'I' for Imprimeries and 'F' for Fournisseurs,' she explained. The upside was that it helped all of our non-French-speaking staff learn a lot of new vocabulary very quickly!

Of course files are really there to decorate your office walls or cupboards! Their principal function is to gather dust. So you need to clean them out every so often. I took this to extremes last year and hired one of those builder's skips. I filled it in half a day with old management books, research papers and the like. Hoarding is OK as long as it is useful. I have research material from two decades ago that I quite often find useful. So when you have that office clearout, think carefully about what goes and what stays. You can be too tidy.

I tend to file by project, allocating every project a number. These act as current project files (I use simple clear plastic folders with a sticker label to indicate the project), and then are just filed away when the project is complete. Ongoing projects (for example, I research and write monthly and quarterly newsletters for clients) usually have a master file that contains basic agreements, meeting discussions and ideas as well as a file for each edition of the newsletter (used for research notes, draft and final copies). Like many consultants, I have my own idiosyncratic habits. In my case nothing gets issued a number until the work is confirmed, otherwise I feel I am tempting fate. Superstitious? You bet!

In addition, I keep client contracts, proposals and customer contracts in the client's file and in a master file as well. That way you can usually lay your hands on a copy fairly quickly.

**3** **TIP** I'm old-fashioned in some things. So while I appreciate the freedom that technology has given me, I still like a piece of paper. If like me, you tend to forget to back up your computer every Friday before you pack it in for the weekend, make sure that all those proposals and contracts and confidentiality agreements are in hard copy format and filed away, preferably in a safe (see below).

# The production plan

I have always – since the day I started working as an independent consultant (25 September 1982 to be exact) – run my business from a production plan. The reason for this was probably that in my employed career, most of the firms I worked for operated in that way. While it helps everyone in a firm keep track of who is doing what and meeting deadlines, it is also an invaluable aid for the solo worker. Although the idea of having a planning meeting with yourself may sound a little bizarre, it does pay off. Most of all it imposes a certain discipline which over time becomes second nature.

What I have done regarding the production plan is to rigorously stick to two rules:

1 It must be updated each week (no matter where I am).
2 It has to fit on a single page only (which is why mine is currently in 8pt type!).

I have an electronic copy with me wherever I go, but a hard-copy sits on one of the plastic document holders next to my big flat screen and there will be a hard-copy with me when I travel.

Every Monday morning (just as I did with my team for many years) I have a planning session – but now, with myself. I find that if I don't do this, there are certain things I never follow up on. That is why it is there. It tells me about the big projects I have on the go, but it also reminds me of the opportunities I need to chase. That is its real value to me. I know what I have to do each week, but what I need is a reminder for those longer-term actions.

I call mine a production plan and indeed it does examine the things in progress. But it is also my key *aide-mémoire* for the things I need to keep an eye on. From this production plan meeting with myself, I develop a 'To Do' list for that day and the week to come.

So what's on Mike Johnson's one-page production plan?

> **Current booked business**: This comprises projects that have been agreed (and given a project number as explained earlier). To that are added certain basic details: state of project (including completed, billed but not paid: they only come off when they are paid in full!), subject for a newsletter, next client meet, deadline date, etc.

> **Business Development: The Critical List:** These are the projects I am currently bidding for (usually that means a proposal is under consideration). It includes what the project is and its current status.

> **Business Development**: Follow-ups: These comprise hot and not so hot contacts that you really need (both as possible business opportunities but also for research and networking opportunities).

> **Meeting/Conference Commitments**: Where I am supposed to be and what I am speaking on and related issues.

> **The Future Work Forum**: Events and issues related to the network I have created.

> **The Percentage Club**: Details of the co-workers I have business development/referral agreements with and their current status.

> **Personal Writing**: Current 'Mike Johnson' only projects (like this book).

> **Upcoming Visits**: Details of people I need to contact when I travel to different cities.

Without my production plan I would be lost. Personally, I have never found another way to keep all of my activities in one place that is so effective and simple to use. This is not a to-do list, it is an easy to update summary of my professional life. Incidentally, if you keep hard or electronic copies for a period of years, it is a great way to track how your business developed and evolved and how clients waxed and waned. A potted corporate history of your business – one page at a time.

# Set a routine

I have referred a great deal to the need to have a plan. This equally applies to how you intend to work on a day-to-day basis. One of the big dangers of working for yourself is that the lines between on-time and off-time begin to blur. If you are working from home, it is all too easy to wander into your 'office' in your bathrobe at 5 am because you can't sleep, do a few things at the weekend and 'just check for that e-mail' at 10 pm before you turn in for the night. For some of us it doesn't matter. For others, it really is necessary to create a routine.

When you were in that 9 to 5 job there was a routine to the place you worked. In fact it was probably so routine that you never really noticed it after the first couple of weeks. Well that's what you have to create in your new life. Having a routine helps keep the wheels on, especially in those early days. Breaking for a coffee, taking a quick walk, having lunch. Pacing your day like that will help you create your own pace of working.

I need to confess that I am writing this in my (very comfortable) office at 22.00 hrs on a Friday evening. Reason, I'm enjoying myself! But that works for me, would it work for you?

And though creating the basic routine is important, the pace you set is vital too. If things are quiet you can do one of two things: (a) get worried and go searching desperately for new business or (b) go have a good lunch. I am not joking. I like what I call 'down-days' when you know that however hard you try, the people you call won't be there (of course they are employees, so they are 'in a meeting'), promised material doesn't arrive and plans take a last-minute dive into the abyss. At this point you may as well store up your energies and creative juices and head for the nearest hostelry. The strange thing is that every time I do that, I take my big pad of legal paper and I always get at least one good idea. So don't sit alone and mope about, get out and see the world – it really makes a difference.

Then there is the other side of the independent consultant's coin – the day all hell breaks loose, the heavens fall in and there's a five alarm fire burning on your desk. And this cataclysmic event always takes place the day before you go on vacation or on your wife's birthday/your daughter's wedding/first school play/graduation (choose one). My view on this is that there is always tomorrow. Go and do what you need to do (the family obligation) and then clear up the mess. You may spend the day traumatised about how you are going to pay for your daughter's wedding when you think you may have just blown the Acme Engineering account, but it seldom comes to that (honest!).

On those other days when the alarm bell rings as you are preparing to switch off the lights – well that's show business. That's what you signed up for. At times like this it is useful to remind yourself (and your nearest and dearest too) that if you were still an employee you wouldn't just be down the hallway or across the garden. You would still be at work, but faced with having to switch the lights back on, and with a late-night commute into the bargain.

In a two-decade consulting career, I have pulled all sorts of late-night fire-fighting stints and client hand-holding gigs. It comes with many of the jobs we choose to do. Often it will bring you closer to your clients, make you a much better consultant and enhance your reputation. I have found that it usually leads to more work from a grateful client.

# Set the pattern for YOUR work ethic

So you have to ask yourself the big question: why are you spending these lonely days and nights trying to make this idea of yours work? Let's get back to that plan of yours that needs constant updating and revision. What are those objectives and rules you set up for yourself? One of them is getting clients to understand how YOU work. To get them on board in this, setting a behaviour pattern is vital. Clients can and do use and abuse independent consultants fairly brutally at times. So you need to set some ground rules that – without being articulated too directly – are very, very clear all the same. If you are seen to drop everything, change plans just because they need to see you, they will feed on this insecurity. Never, ever let that happen. Very often the solution is as simple as taking your client aside and explaining that you do have other commitments. While stating that you value their business highly, you need to convey the fact that you are not 'employed' exclusively by them. Indeed, it is the very range of your business that makes you a valuable asset as you are constantly up to date with the latest developments and thinking in their industry. Maybe you should let them know that more often.

Now I know (because we have all been there) that when you are scratching around like a chicken in a barnyard for business, taking a tough line with a client can seem hard to do, but it is good advice. Give in too early and when you look back later you will regret it.

> **TIP** When there's little business in the offing it is easy to say 'Yes, Yes, Yes' to anything. Unless you are about to go out of business and start selling the family silver, don't do it. You're bound to regret it later.

Sure there are some really horrid people out there who will try and use you – but most won't. If you do a good job, most clients will take the trouble to listen and at least make an attempt to understand – you wish!

Of course, just about anyone who has stayed the course for two decades has grabbed at one of those tempting offers, when business has been in the doldrums. I have done it myself. Did I regret it? Yes I did! Did I do anything about it? Oh yes. As soon as we were back in funds I fired the client. If you have never done it, let me tell you that there is nothing more satisfying than firing a client – it produces a golden glow inside that lasts for quite a time – at least until you can't pay next month's invoices.

These are the times that no one (until now) ever tells you about. The dark days when you need a certain resilience to keep going. Virtually everyone I know has had these and you need a great deal of confidence and self-belief to keep on going. You may recall that I explained that sometimes you need a shoulder to cry on – these are the times.

There will be times when you will work on projects you don't like and don't believe in for the very basic reason that there isn't much else you can do. It is the independent's version of, in corporate life, getting a new boss and discovering mutual hatred. The only outcome is to knuckle down and get on with it – and then get out as swiftly and cleanly as you can.

The upside? Yes, there is always an upside. In this case you will have learned a lot. And that sort of experience is extremely valuable in helping you to survive in the future.

## Missing your mates and cabin fever

To compound the trauma of going it alone, there are the twin terrors of missing your mates and cabin fever. It isn't until you actually sit in that chair in your new 'office' for a week that it really dawns on you what you have done. Days can be long. Depending on the kind of consulting you are doing, there can be extensive periods when you are – literally – working on your own. Certainly most of us spend time outside our self-created cabinet of horrors, but it takes a good three to six months to begin to get the hang of really being alone.

Over the years, those making the transition from employee to solo worker have listed these as some of the major things they miss about not being surrounded by other co-workers:

> **Loss of office social life**: Few of us realise until it is too late that the sandwich around the corner, the coffee or glass of wine after

work are key parts of the working day. The answer to this is to look around where you are working now and see if you can find alternatives. Chances are, that unless you are in the Outer Hebrides, there is going to be a like-minded person fairly close by.

> **Loss of colleagues' expertise**: This can be really tough. The interaction we have come to take for granted is suddenly not there. My advice is try to stay in touch with some of your old colleagues or make brutal (short-term) use of your support network to talk with and try out ideas.

> **Feeling 'trapped' at home 24 hours a day**: Where consultants have major projects this kind of cabin fever can assume serious levels. Like anything else, you have to learn to recognise it and destroy it. Make a point of just taking a walk – even for 15 minutes each morning and afternoon. I take the dog out and also talk to it for most of the time, if I am cooped up. I am a great believer in dogs and cats in the solo worker's environment.

> **Reduced training opportunities**: You never miss it until it isn't there. Now staying ahead and up-to-speed is all about personal responsibility and personal cost. The danger is, if you don't invest in your own knowledge, your skills will get out of date very fast and so you'll be less marketable.

> **Reduced equipment facilities**: When you had that 'job', you had all the hardware and software you would ever need. Now you are responsible for that all by yourself. Clients move rapidly up the software curve and you need to do the same. It is very embarrassing not to be able to download because you haven't got the latest update. Worse still, you know nothing about IT. Why? Because the man from technical services always showed up. Where is he now?

> **Poor working facilities**: Face it, MegaCorps' offices were pretty cool weren't they? That noodle bar and Starbucks in reception and the free magazines, games and DVDs were to die for. Now, it is all on you. So, make your new work environment the very best you can (see Chapter 9).

> **Reduced information input**: Like a lack of colleagues' expertise and being cut off from training, you just don't get the information that keeps you up to date any more. So seek out new ways. Take a coffee break and surf the net. Find and create favourite places that will keep you going. Subscribe to magazines, go to shows, network and keep in touch with old colleagues (pick up the phone now).

# The partner and the kids

We have touched on this before, but we really need to visit it again. Because, when you begin to work from home, those rules about creating a personal, secure space can go quickly out of the window. This is especially true if cabin fever does set in, or you miss someone to talk to. It is all too easy to sneak in to the kitchen for a cup of coffee and a little dialogue. But you can't give in to that. Call your 'shoulder-to-cry-on' mates by all means, but stick it out. You have to establish not just in your mind, but in the minds of everyone else around you that what you are doing is paramount. And top of that list is the physical separation you are able to create on a day-to-day basis.

Looking back over the years, I realise that for the majority of my solo-working career, my friends and most of their partners had little understanding of what I did, and frankly didn't show much more than a very casual passing interest. The fact that you will possibly be worried about how this great adventure you have embarked upon is going to turn out will tend to make you irritable and short tempered too. So hopefully, those closest to you will spend a large part of the day avoiding you as much as possible. It may be at this time that you wished you'd taken that little shared office on the High Street, even if it was over your budget. Indeed, finding out what you actually do can come as something of a shock to the rest of your family or your partner, especially if you are taking over – and ring-fencing – parts of the home you share. I know we all hear about couples who are totally compatible and are going to create a great business together. Well, in my experience those are created by Hollywood scriptwriters and have no bearing on cold reality.

I knew a very austere, precise Scandinavian consultant who described this working-from-home discovery process as 'the moment that the home becomes a machine for working in, when the norms and expectations for social life at home are challenged.' He went on to say that, 'at this point it does seem necessary to establish an etiquette for working within the domestic scene, regarding the division between work and leisure.' That's what I call a sensible, diplomatic Norwegian way of saying, 'Stay out of my space until 6 o'clock or else.'

What you are doing as a home worker is just as much a strange alien experience for your partner/family as it is for you. If you have children, they will find it difficult to realise that Daddy or Mummy is home all day. Moreover, they will find it difficult to accept that you are actually working. As I said in Chapter 2, set those 'stay out' of my office rules early and stick with them through thick and thin.

But, having asked you to be really hard-assed about this, expect to see some disruption too. This isn't just a new experience for you, it's equally strange for everyone around you. To add to your stress, they will delight in telling you their views on how all this is working out. How do you deal with this? By being honest. Explain that you are trying hard, and that you do need space to get your job done. If, after a few months it doesn't work out, find an alternative somewhere.

> **5** **TIP:** If you find it impossible to create the right space at home, a small office will be a small price to pay for having an environment where you can really get down to work.

## The social v. business thing

There seem to be very few independent consultants who are able to totally separate their professional and private lives (that's why a lot of people find it impossible and prefer the black and white lifestyle that a 9 to 5 job offers). Certainly, most of us have to get used to some grey areas when we work from the family home. As I pointed out earlier, it isn't just the family, it is the 'buzz' that surrounds most households one way or another that many find the most distracting. But there is another part, the other side of the coin – not being able to stop working.

For this new venture to succeed in the long term, it really is important that you are able to switch off and have a private life. What you have to do is set rules so you don't find yourself at the beck and call of clients at all hours of the day and night. Equally, you need to know when to call it a day and turn out the lights.

Admittedly, when you are trying to build up a business, it's difficult to turn people away, but sometimes you need to for your own – and possibly your partner's – sanity. That is why (see Chapter 9) I advocate strongly – if you work from home – having a separate entrance from the outside into your workspace. Even if it means knocking a hole in the wall to accommodate an entrance door. Not only is this a more professional solution if your clients need to visit, but it also clearly separates your business and social arrangements.

Outside of your home, of course, it is practically impossible to have a real separation barrier between your work and your play time. If you are working in a specific community (as a local accountant, for example), your business life and social life will naturally run in parallel for much of the time.

Equally, if you are another sort of professional (personal trainer, business consultant) you will probably need to spend 'investment' time with clients, which is a social activity. Indeed, throughout my career as an independent consultant, many of my clients have come through a social meeting. And the more people that take up solo working as a means to earn a living, the more the social and professional lines will blur.

Looking at it from another angle, most of the people you will end up working with as a solo operator will be people you like, trust and admire for their professional skills. This is one of the great advantages of working for yourself. You get to choose your co-workers. Clients can be a different thing entirely! But even there, the ones you really don't like – or conversely, don't like you – rarely last very long. Subconsciously we all seem able to move on from the people we really don't enjoy working with. Having said that, there's no point in being silly and juvenile about clients that you don't like. In the early days at least, you'll find that putting up with a difficult client is a whole lot better than having sleepless nights over your income stream.

> **TIP** You don't have to be good friends with all your clients. If one or two of them are difficult or over-demanding, just stay very focused and professional. Do the job the best way possible and keep a little distance. Often you'll find this is not about you, just the way they like to work with everyone.

## Taking time off

When you start up an independent business, it is hard to think of vacation time. Your purpose in life is to get established and create a viable operation that can support you and whoever else is part of your life. All of us have had those moments when we say, 'I just can't afford to go away, what happens if...?' Well, a very old friend of mine changed my mind on this, by applying a piece of very subtle psychology. 'Just imagine,' he said, 'that you had to go to the US or some other distant location for some meetings. You'd take a week out, wouldn't you?' Well, you don't need to lie to your clients if you want to take a week off, just say that you are going travelling.'

And from that day on, that's what I have done. At the beginning of each year, I block out the weeks when I am 'travelling'. OK, there may be a time every so often when something destroys the plan, but basically if you tell people you are going to be away that week it is accepted. The uncool way to do it is the Friday morning before you depart. Then there will ALWAYS be an emergency.

**TIP** If you don't travel much for work there are always training weeks, professional conferences and other reasons for 'travelling'.

Once clients understand that you are not there 365 days a year, they will quickly 'get' it. And if they don't? Well, you're lucky. The total acceptance and ease of e-mail, conference calls and guaranteed overnight delivery means that most of us can work efficiently from anywhere, staying connected at the same time.

But you do need to get away. Breaks are good for the soul. In start-up mode, you are all too open to working long hours, rushing meals and not having the time to just sit and think. If your partner suggests you need a break, listen to them – they probably know what they are talking about. Although I cover a great deal more about being in touch on the road in Chapter 10, when you go 'travelling' make sure people can reach you easily. When I am on vacation I always have my mobile phone with me, and usually a lap-top as well. And it is always useful to know the location of the nearest Internet café (even if you have no plans to use it). These days I use a professional answering service when I go into holiday mode. For a small fee I get my calls to the office diverted, seamlessly, and a voice answers using my company name. Then once a day, or once a week they give me by e-mail, fax or phone a list of the calls.

If it is a period of intense activity, I will call in once a day. But if my answering service knows how to reach me, I rarely call in more than once a week. Let's face it, if something really does blow up, all your clients should know your mobile number, and they won't be scared to use it.

**TIP** When going on vacation, call the hotel in advance and see if you can get Internet access and use of a PC at the location. It saves you carrying a lap-top with you. Equally, if you are using a villa or apartment, ask the rental company what facilities they have. And, too often overlooked, ask whether there any known 'dead zones' where mobile phone reception is poor or non-existent.

## Playing the percentage game

Often I get asked by individuals contemplating a leap into the unknown world of the independent, what is the optimum breakdown of time (e.g. how much on production, how much on prospecting for business, etc.)?

The answer to that is another of life's great mysteries. It depends entirely on the type of consulting you are going to do. Some consultants never have to go at looking for business, it just comes in. Neither do they ever have to market themselves, all their business comes from word of mouth. I should warn you though, this state of affairs is very rare. Sooner or later market conditions conspire to change even the most rock-solid consulting proposition. Changing business trends, new competition coming into the market, technological breakthroughs – all these can conspire to upset a cosy world a consultant has built up so assiduously. I have met many self-satisfied consultants who have told me they never need to go looking for business. My bet is that sooner or later they will – and the more arrogant they are about how clever they seem, the sooner that will happen.

How you divide up your day or week is tied entirely to the type of business you are going to be involved in and the variety and intensity of the work. That said, unless you are very, very lucky (even if you are very, very good), there are going to be times when business goes a little slack – general economic downturns whack consultants like everyone else. When that moment comes it is too late to moan about what you should have done. You need to get out there and think about creating new business.

You need to spend a certain percentage of your work time, week in, week out looking for future work, or 'priming the pump' as it is called. In my case, while I have some regular assignments, few go on for ever (circumstances and people change too much for that, especially in today's world). Also, in my case much of the work I do is based on a project that has a distinct beginning, middle and end. While you may be able to prolong the end, because there is often some unplanned activity that wasn't in the initial brief, there is usually a sense of finality. At that point you need to have that pump primed for more business.

Now I know it is difficult when you are busy to stop and begin looking for the next business, but you have to do it and make it a habit. All successful independent consultants do this rigorously and with a focused regularity that would probably surprise those that have never been in this position. And the more you do it, the better you get at seeing opportunities.

Taking a five-day week as a norm, I would suggest that to maintain a proper flow of business in normal economic times, you need to spend 20 per cent of your time (one day out of five) on new business development. Now if you are sitting fat and sassy, up to your ears in business you are probably shaking your head, thinking 'no, no, no, I don't need this.' There is a very simple answer to that: YES, YES, YES, YOU DO! I don't know anyone, who has ever survived past that 24-month watershed, who hasn't assiduously prospected for business. Just as employees get made redundant, so independent consultants get similar treatment.

So plan for 20 per cent in good times (one day a week), and up to 40 per cent at other times. You'll soon learn how to judge what you've got in the pipeline and how long it will last. And please remember that just because you write a proposal doesn't mean that it will automatically translate into work. Proposals are like promises, few come to fruition. If your scoring rate is above 40 per cent, you are doing well.

### THE ONE-THIRD, ONE-THIRD, ONE-THIRD MODEL

Sometimes a good dose of cynicism goes a long way to keep us independents alive. One work colleague of mine suggests that the more accurate breakdown for any independent today is 1/3, 1/3, 1/3. This she explains as one-third of your time to get business; one-third of the time to carry out the assignment; and the final one-third trying to get paid by the client. Don't laugh, it's serious and you would do well to reflect on the fact that this is what can happen and you need to be ready for it. There is no point at being good at getting business and at delivering a quality product or project if you stall at getting paid quickly.

Business development and marketing yourself involve all types of activity. This can include networking, events, visits to clients and prospects, marketing activity through mail, Internet and so forth. It can include writing articles, giving speeches and making yourself as visible as possible (Chapters 6 and 7 cover this in detail). It can be a matter of taking the right contact out for lunch or a drink.

But do it, and have a plan for it. Many of us, certainly in the early years as we struggle to get established and develop a reputation, do much of this activity out of mainstream business hours or at weekends. But to help you to get a true picture of your working week, you should keep a time sheet.

# Keeping time sheets

In a lot of professions, time sheets are the way of accounting and therefore charging for the time we spend on a client's business. But what I am advocating here is to keep a rolling time sheet on everything you do in the business. Log all the calls and e-mails that you make or receive. Log the time you work on client business, the time you take off for 'thinking' time or a coffee/sandwich break. Log all the time you are idle as well, you'll be quite surprised how much of that there really is.

If you do that for a month, you'll begin to build up an honest picture of your overall commercial activity. My bet is that you will probably astound yourself just how much time you waste. I had a work colleague who discovered that he was wasting about two days in every five. So he replanned his business day and took the time off instead!

By keeping careful track of what you 'really' do, you will begin to get a true picture of your working life, and how you might improve. It is the one way of getting a truly transparent look at your activities. In case this idea appears to be a really boring chore, I am not suggesting you do this for ever, just until you get an honest picture of how you spend your working day. All the same, it does pay to go back from time to time and do it over.

> **9 TIP** Put the time sheet onto an Excel spreadsheet and open it up every day. That way you can simply click and record. You can also get into the ritual of tidying it up every night before you log off.

## Never put all your beans in one tin

This may be the postmodern version of eggs in a basket, but it sounds a little more contemporary. My point here is that I have seen too many independents (even those with three, four or more employees) getting it terribly wrong by putting virtually all their business with one client. The client rarely knows that you have – in reality – bet the farm on his future. YOU do and you shouldn't be doing it.

It is all too easy to go down this route. You start work, you get a really good client, they give you more and more work. You even think that the work has diversified, because you are now working for this group and that group, division A and division B and so on. Wake up! You are working for the same company. You may have actually done what we talked about and primed that new business pump. And where better to do it than somewhere you can get easy access to others, who feel comfortable with you, because you already work with their colleagues? This is not business development; it's business evolvement (which we will talk about in the next chapter).

Today's business world is a cruel, fast-changing and unforgiving place. And it doesn't matter where or how you work, as that famous phrase has it, 'shit happens'. And if we have all our beans piled up in one tin, they are going to get burned – badly – when things get hot.

Here are two stories that explain why evolving your business inside one firm is not a good idea. These are real stories, take heed or it could happen to you.

> **Case 1**: Two work colleagues set themselves up in a new, shiny consulting firm together. They quickly land a dream client: a large, expanding international corporation. As the client grows so do they, taking on people, expanding the offices. Although they did have other business, the rest of their clients take second place. Within three years 90 plus per cent of all their business comes from the one major client (but it is split across industries, divisions and geographies). Then one day, the whole dream turns into a nightmare. The company they had toiled so loyally for is taken over in a surprise acquisition. Within six months they have no business, it has all devolved to the new owner's in-house and external support.

> **Case 2**: A highly successful marketing consulting firm (of three partners) becomes the *de facto* in-house cross-border marketing team for a large US multinational's operations in Europe. Gradually this multinational giant becomes virtually the only client. One day, the president, Europe, who had championed this small creative group, leaves the business. The new incumbent (by nature a cost-cutter) issues a series of edicts within 48 hours of getting into the job. One of these is 'no external consultants, under any circumstances'. The rest, as they say, is not a nice story.

You can't predict the future. We are all vulnerable. As independents at the time we feel the most secure, we are the most vulnerable, because we have probably reached the zenith of that relationship. Rule to follow every day – prime the pump, develop, develop, develop. Allow one day a week for this – even when (especially when) you're busy.

And it doesn't matter whether you are working in a local, national or international market context. Things change. Not only do they change, they change quickly and very finally. Consider these scenarios and try and look out for them, although most of the time they take even the best operators by surprise.

> The bottom, literally, falls out of a market. Everyone in that industry is having a really bad time. You are no longer a solution, you are a cost. *Advice*: Try, wherever possible, to work across a range of industries. Usually, they don't all take a dive together.

> Mergers and acquisitions can quickly and seriously affect your small business. When one company buys another, consolidation doesn't just take place inside – they usually cut 50 per cent of the external suppliers too.

> ➤ Changes of management. The CEO, CFO or HR director you have so carefully cultivated over the years is suddenly gone. It is time to start all over again.

So, watch carefully. Nothing in this business is for ever, no matter how good it looks today.

> **10 TIP** Don't rely on departing personnel to give you work in their next company either. While it can happen, all too often they take time to get into a position to do this or inherit an already efficient and knowledgeable external support infrastructure. Remember the rule: you can't eat promises.

## Staying fit

With all this worry about getting a business off the ground and then – when it is finally running like a well-oiled machine – being concerned if it will all implode, it is amazing that we aren't all thin, twitching, stressed-out wrecks. The thing is, if you haven't got some resilience you won't start life as a consultant in the first place. Luckily, it isn't all doom and gloom. Certainly, there will be some low points, but we have just got to make the best of those and move on. That's what independents do.

Oh, and another thing. Remember paranoia? In Chapter 1 I suggested that a good dose of paranoia goes a long way. Well, if you are a fully paid-up, totally paranoid independent you will play client melt-down scenarios in your head. Surprising just how much paranoid thinking – 'What happens if they have a bad year/get taken over/ don't like this latest proposal'? – can help you spot a forthcoming train wreck before anyone else.

However, being fit (obviously not mentally as you can see from above!) adds a great deal to that resilience and ability to get up and go. The one thing an independent consultant can't afford is to have a serious illness. The theory of an 'ounce of prevention' was never truer than in this profession. Remember, you are all you've got. You are not the greatest asset the firm has, you are the ONLY asset. There is just you and your intellectual property and, sadly, no one can use that on your behalf. What is your unique offering is also your Achilles heel. Unlike a shopkeeper or a manufacturer, people can't sell the stock of your business – YOU – unless you are there. Therefore, taking care of yourself is of paramount importance.

First you need to stay fit. Not Olympian fit, I hasten to add, but fit and healthy. A long-standing colleague of mine says that he makes a point – whatever else is happening – of having two good sessions at the gym each week. Me, I walk the dog – often long distances. It doesn't matter what you do but you need to make sure you are able to get up and go. In fact, you may find that you spend – in your new role – longer hours sitting than you did as an employee. You don't walk to the station for your commute any more, you don't walk to lunch. If you don't have some sort of exercise regime it is possible the only parts of your body that get any exercise are your fingers on that keyboard – carpal tunnel syndrome here we come!

Part of this pacing yourself that I talked about is primarily about taking breaks. So many of us these days spend a large part of our lives at a workstation staring at a VDU, that we do need to get up a stretch every so often. Those exercises that long-haul airline operators now advise you do on their flights are the kind of thing I mean. If you are not up for that, then just getting up every hour or so and crossing the room to put the kettle on, or a similar activity prevents you staying locked in one position for too long.

Fitness is also watching what you eat. It is all too easy – especially if your office is part of the family home – to snack from the fridge or sabotage the biscuit supply. DON'T. Try to get the kind of diet that makes it easy for you to work. If you can't help snacking, eat fruit. You need to be able to work long and hard at times, travel and meet people. So mobility and the ability to think clearly for long periods are vital.

## Health checks

Whatever your age, make sure you consult your doctor on a regular basis – and your dentist. If you need to have things done, get them done. Otherwise they always happen when you are at your busiest or, worse still, travelling. Also, I have never seen a successful independent consultant with bad teeth! Think about it.

## Health and work insurance

Your time is precious. That is all you have and you can't afford to waste it on the wrong things. So get good health insurance that covers you 365 days a year wherever you may be and your travel as well. My own experience is that if it looks really cheap, the service and the result will be too.

Get the best insurance you can afford; if nothing else, it will give you peace of mind. Also, I advise a professional insurance that will pay out if you lose the ability to work. Consider how much you need to live comfortably and then insure yourself for that. It won't be cheap, but it will provide a security net if something really bad happens.

Hunt around for health and particularly travel insurance, as you can easily pay too much. Find good private cover that works in the country you operate from. Then supplement that with a really good travel insurance (be wary of discount travel insurance offers). Many of the best are available from the major banks (where you already use their other services anyway) or the major credit card companies.

# Saving for the future

Yes, you need to do it, but the options are endless. My advice is talk to your accountant, banker or independent financial adviser. Also get a second opinion and even a third opinion before you plunge in. Too many so-called financial advisers have been proved wrong these last years. Whatever you do, don't put all the beans in the same tin. Try to tuck something away for a rainy day that no one knows about. Just in case; call it emergency rations.

# Getting an office supplier

Sorry, you'll have to go to Chapter 9 for this. But, in start-up mode, think carefully about what you really need to buy. You won't need anything like as much as you think you do. My bet is that if you go on a shopping spree at some office supply company or order online, two years later you'll have a cupboard full of unused and unwanted paraphernalia.

# Finding professional advice: financial, legal, IT

Good suppliers can, and often do, determine just how successful you will be. Rule one is very straightforward. For professional advice (financial, legal and IT) get the best that you can decently afford. If you go and see an accountant who immediately tells you how much he is going to save you and how much tax you won't have to pay – leave.

## Financial advice

You do need a good **accountant**. I have never found good accountants any more expensive than bad ones. If you find yours is bad, fire them quickly. It may seem like a pain but it will pay off later. And I don't mean just bad advice. Being slow with your tax returns, never available, that's the type you need to avoid. For more on corporate taxation, VAT, national insurance, pensions, etc. see Chapter 11 and the website accompanying the book: www.pearson-books.com/smarterconsulting.

## Legal advice

You may need a good **law firm**. Not because you expect to get involved in legal wrangling, but to give quick, friendly and timely advice when it is needed. That sort of advice seems to be always needed in a hurry, so the time to appoint a good law firm is before you really need them. Also, it is a good place for filing papers of incorporation of the business, getting official papers notarised and so forth. Then again, if some nasty and unforeseen event does happen (remember we do live in an increasingly litigious society), it is good to know there is someone just a call away who knows at least the basics of your business.

## Banking services

A **bank** is a must-have. Choose the one in your area that has the best total services. Go for one initially that will open free business accounts and give you lots of free services – at least in the first 12 months. *Advice*: keep your personal finances and your professional finances well apart. That means get a business account, with a cash and credit card. Also get a card that offers virtually unlimited credit if you need it and that also gives you lots of points/airmiles. Get to know the manager and see if you can run a line of credit if required. If you are doing international business, see what they offer between Euro, Sterling, Swiss franc and US dollar accounts. These types of service – and local banker's experience and knowledge of it – vary widely, so you may need to shop around.

## IT support

In these technologically driven days, you need a good **IT adviser**. This will depend on the size of your business and how much you know and can handle confidently yourself. If you are small, get someone who is also small, but has some leverage when it comes to building and buying the equipment (hardware and software) that you need. Most important, they need to be close by. If you have a mega-virus feasting on your hard drive, you need someone who can be there fast. These days you cannot afford to have downtime. Clients can and do have downtime, their suppliers DO NOT!

I am continually amazed by the inability of some independents (usually older ones) to grasp the need for good IT back-up. Worse still, those that seem to spend hours trying to fix IT problems themselves. For some reason it seems like a huge victory to have taken a day to solve a systems crash that an IT professional could have solved in half an hour. Back to the beginning of the book: don't waste time on things that you're not good at – it isn't smart or professional.

> **11 TIP** As with everything else, don't go for a cheap IT assistance provider, because you'll get a cheap – and often wrong – solution. Try them out on a few things first and see how quickly they can fix a problem. You don't care about what they are doing as long as they get you up and running fast.

### Webmaster

Equally, unless you are very good at this sort of thing yourself, appoint a **webmaster** who can make sure that your website stays up to date. I know a lot of older independent consultants who have clearly failed to embrace the coming of the digital age. Not having a website is one. Frankly I doubt that I will ever get much business from having a well-maintained site. But what it does is explain who I am and what I do. Its main function for my business is to allow people to check me out. Particularly when I am doing research, I find that while I am on the phone, people are online checking up on who I am and how legitimate my business really is. Websites are increasingly important. They are the company brochure of the twenty-first century (except a lot cheaper to produce and update). Again, be careful who you hire for this role. Personally I value technical competence over undisciplined creativity.

## Other suppliers

Depending on your business, there are many other suppliers that could be critical, such as **printers, transport firms, couriers, travel agents, leasing firms, insurance brokers**. In all cases, ask around, find who uses different organisations and why. Often services are widely variable – even by big operators – from region to region.

> **12** **TIP** Get a monthly account with your local taxi firm. It means you can get around town, to railways stations and airports without having to think about cash. Also they are useful for picking up clients and ferrying documents around as required, when you are really pressed for time.

## Insurance

Make sure that your office (even if it is part of your home) is adequately insured, specifically any high-value contents. Also ensure that any equipment that you regularly travel with (e.g. phones, lap-tops and cameras) are fully covered. But do shop around, rates very hugely, and from year to year. Some insurance firms frown on home offices and will certainly demand that they are separately insured otherwise the house and contents insurance can be null and void if something happens. Make sure that you are adequately protected by making certain that your home insurance provider knows that you use it for professional purposes.

Hopefully you are now in the right frame of mind to get started. Good. For the next step, we are going to examine how to sell yourself, how you begin to create business and maintain and evolve those vital client relationships.

## Key learning points

> ➤ You must find ways to get that administration done – don't leave it. If you can afford it, get someone to help you.

> ➤ If you get busy and are out of the office a lot, a 'helper' makes sense too.

> ➤ Bank direct debits save you getting cut-off from vital services (e.g. phone and electric) if you travel a lot.

> ➤ Save time: pile up all your payments and do them once a month.

> ➤ Same goes for invoicing: don't forget to get it out on time or you won't get paid.

- Always get at least one-third of the project budget up front.
- Have a production plan as a guide to current business and future opportunities and update it weekly.
- Learn to pace your day – don't become a workaholic. Get out, take a walk, exercise.
- Everyone has down-days. Don't sit and mope about – go treat yourself to a coffee or 'sneak' off to lunch, you'll feel better.
- Don't abandon important personal milestones or family obligations to fight fires – you'll regret it later if you do.
- Learn how to take vacations.
- Don't forget you need that shoulder to cry on.
- Feeling trapped at home and getting 'cabin fever' are normal. Just learn to get out and do other things.
- Remember to set rules on your work-space so you are not interrupted.
- You'll be spending a lot of time in your new 'office', so make sure that it's an enjoyable working space.
- Never forget to prime the pump – 20 per cent of work time on business development.
- No matter how enticing it looks, never, ever work for only one client – it is long-term suicide.
- Make sure you stay healthy: exercise, eat well, watch that diet.
- Find good suppliers: accountant, law firm, bank, IT support and a webmaster if you can't do it yourself.
- Get insured, yourself and your business – you know it makes sense.

# Chapter **5**

# The life of a salesman

'Whenever you're sitting across from some important person, always picture them sitting in their underwear. That's the way I always operated in business.'

**Joseph P. Kennedy**

'The customer's always right,
The son of a bitch
Is probably rich
So smile with all your might.'

**Noel Coward**

To a great extent, this chapter is probably the most important of all. Why? Well, if you can't sell yourself, your product or your service, no great idea, genius level IQ, hard work, smart offices or a really well-organised administrative system are going to do you any good at all. Being perfectly honest, if you can't sell you don't eat. Please don't confuse selling with marketing either (that comes in the next chapter). We are talking about the bald, bad business of selling. In this case, yourself. The other thing to get clear right now is that marketing yourself (or your business) happens in a carefully considered way, selling doesn't. You can do it two ways only:

> face-to-face (which is best)
> on the phone.

Think about it this way: selling, real selling, is one thing and one thing only – a contact sport. It should be in the Olympics for goodness sake!

And that is why so many people can't do it, can never, ever get to grips with it. If you have worked inside a company and just done a job, no one has probably ever asked you to sell something. If you have worked in a big consulting firm, you have probably been fed work – no one ever said, 'Go and see Client X and sell him or her something.'

So when you take the plunge, put the brass plaque up on the door, you may be well qualified at what you do, you may know lots of stuff. But you are quite possibly at a distinct disadvantage, you've never sold anything to anyone!

In more than two decades of selling myself most days in one way or another, I have seen so many highly successful people fail on this very basic issue of being unable to sell effectively. And this is the critical point – no doubt about that. If you can't get comfortable and find your own way to get people to say 'yes', then it doesn't matter what kind of genius you are – it just won't work. On the other hand, if you 'get it', then life is going to be good. The buzz of being able to sell is wonderful (even more so when you are selling yourself).

I've looked at this critical watershed in any independent's life time after time and to my mind there are four pillars of failure – points or attitudes where it really goes wrong. If you recognise yourself in one of these, please think long and hard about your next step.

## Selling failure no. 1: you think selling is sleazy

Taking the attitude that selling is a low-life occupation that puts you at the level of a really pushy used car salesman is far more common than you would think. Many good professionals don't realise when they begin the going-it-alone process that the sell is really the key part and a lot of them find it beneath their dignity. Strangely, selling does not come naturally to many of us. There are very few born salesmen and if they are good, they should stick to that and that alone. But for professionals, having to beat a path to a prospective clent is not a natural thing to do.

Many make the huge mistake of thinking that customers will somehow track them down. It won't happen. You need to realise that all the comfort factors of a regular job – the cushions and cosseting – are not there any more. And just as you will have to learn to queue up at the post office to buy your stamps, so you will have to realise that the sell is the key to survival. Can you get over this aversion, this thinking that selling is sleazy? Well some can and some can't. But look at it this way. If you believe fully in yourself, your service, your product, begin by simply telling people what you can do. Don't ask for the order right away (never be too eager), but make it clear that you are a professional. Know what you want (and expect) to charge. Woolly thinking results in very woolly results. You don't have to be a master closer of a sale, just be open, honest and enthusiastic. You can learn the rest.

> **1 TIP** Never, ever leave a sales opportunity without a way back in the next day. Close the door behind you and it stays shut.

## Selling failure no. 2: you forget to sell

Are you shaking your head? Asking, 'What does he mean by that?' Well, every week I see people who get busy and forget to sell (mainly because deep down they don't want to do it anyway). It is so easy to fall into this trap. 'Wow, I'm really busy, I've got to keep at it.' Then one day, you have shipped you last product, written your last report, sent you last invoice and it is another kind of 'Wow' altogether. It is the Wowwwwwwwwwwww, that comes from the echo from the empty store cupboard. Over the years I have seen so many newly minted independents fail because they got busy initially and forgot to prime that pump. No pipeline, no work. And believe me, it is harder to generate work when you have to than when you have a full order book. So no matter how busy you get, devote a set amount of time to business development, and that includes selling (see Chapter 4).

## Selling failure no. 3: you can't ask for the order

This, of course is the classic, which no one wants to admit or talk about, which is why I am bringing it up now. So many of us have a deep-seated psychological hang-up about actually asking for the order. We are not the type of people who have Bob Geldof moments and shout, 'Give us the fucking money!' Most of us – if truth were known – are timid creatures at heart – and we are scared to ask. While a little later in this chapter I'll talk about the psychology of when to ask, you need to realise right from the start that being unable to ask for the order is going to disqualify you from joining the ranks of the sole trader. All the time, I see bright, energetic independents coming a real cropper through their inability to say 'So have you reached a decision yet, can we get started?'

The main reason is clear. It works like this. You have a proposal into the XYZ Group. You've discussed it, modified it, trimmed your fees. You've done everything and you still haven't got the go-ahead. But, as long as you don't ask, they haven't said 'no'. So you wait, for the simple reason that you don't want to hear bad news. Most often, you will find that there are reasons for the delay. But most of all, if you haven't the confidence and the basic chutzpah to push for a decision, that will tell your prospective client that you are not at all sure of yourself. So screw up your courage and make the call. Either way, you will know and you can then get on with your life. Asking for the order can't be avoided – go out and do it. Yes, the best way to do it is face-to-face. Looking a business prospect in the eye is by far the best way.

## Selling failure no. 4: chemistry

Every book about selling says the same thing. When you meet a prospective client, the first 30 seconds determine your ultimate fate. If they like you it's OK. If they don't, you may as well throw in the towel and go home. So the key here is to get to know the signs and get out if you have to as early as you can. No matter how juicy that project may be, if you are honest with yourself, you'll never get it, not in a million years. On the other hand, over my career there are probably hundreds of times when I have got on so well with a prospective client that I have been given more work than I went for (often, much of it I was not even qualified to do!). However, if you keep striking out week after week and you perhaps know that you don't come across well, or don't really like meeting and presenting to new people, maybe this line of work really isn't for you.

But, if you think that you can sell, and have a winning way with prospective clients, let's move on and see what we are going to call your fledgling venture. Or, perhaps more importantly, what or who do you want the market to think you are?

# Oh no! Not another logo!

Over the years I have collected literally thousands of business cards from one-man outfits trying to appear the size of General Motors. Let me give you this tip from the outset: it's a waste of time. Why? Because what people are buying is YOU. Your reputation, your skill. Then again, they also want to feel that you are not totally alone. That you can offer back-up in terms of arms and legs if needed. Yes, I know you are alone, just don't let your clients know that, or at the very least don't emphasise your supreme solo status.

You see, clients don't like to take risks. They want to know that they are dealing with a safe pair of hands that won't spring any surprises. Because of that, they want to be sure that whoever they deal with can deliver under almost any circumstances. In fact, many organisations are banned from signing agreements with solo contractors simply because they can't offer total continuity.

Now you can set yourself up as MegaCorp Inc. and look like you have hundreds of employees, but is that what you really want to convey? My idea, from the outset has been to reassure that I have a suitable network of support around me, but that I am not some huge – therefore expensive – consulting outfit. Anyway, these days, clients can quickly check up on you, so exaggerating on the size of your business is just foolish.

I have found that using my own name, modified to fit the needs of the business, fits the job just fine. No, I don't mean use it as it is but, by a little creativity, make it sound important. Like this:

Johnson & Associates
The Johnson Group
Johnson & Partners
Johnson Consulting

Then attach – for the letterhead, website, business cards and so on – a qualifying line about what you do:

Consultants and Engineers
Accountants and Tax Advisers
Consultants in Corporate Social Responsibility
Defining Marketing Strategy
Changing Corporate Communications

Never, ever make that second line about what you do too limiting or too specific, as you never know in which direction a business opportunity may lead you. You need a flexible, slightly ambiguous title that looks important, yet conveys – unambiguously – what you do as a core consulting business. The rule here is never to tie yourself down. Don't paint yourself into a corner as some super-specialist. As anyone who has been an independent consultant for some years has discovered, you will find your business evolves (not necessarily in the way you plan either).

This uncontrolled metamorphosis of a business happens for two reasons. First, you gain more expertise as you develop and this will lead you to new opportunities. Second, trends are just that and what you may have started out doing has a very definite shelf-life and you need to adapt your offering to suit the changing market. If you lock yourself down with a too tightly defined name and business title, you'll strangle opportunity and diversity.

Of course, you can call yourself the Acme Consulting Group (chances are there is one already), but over the years I have found using your own name and a suitable qualifying descriptor works best, at least in the initial stages.

**2** **TIP** What's your name? Use it.

Having said that, neither do you want to make yourself look too small. So giving yourself a title on the card like Managing Partner, Senior Consultant and the like helps too. It adds weight and gravitas to who you and your business are. This may sound silly to some, but when you are working with clients, you are who you say you are, on your letterhead, your website and your business card. If you publish an article or give a speech, you are who you say you are. It gets reported, it gets read, it becomes YOU. Most of all it helps – reinforces – the sell. And that is what we are trying to achieve. I don't want you to be famous, but I do want you to sell your ideas and skills.

Additionally, being seen as part of some national or international network (real or fictional) gives the whole show a sense of solemn purpose. I know of hundreds of sole traders who have 'relationships' with other consultants and seem to feel that this is all you require to have a letterhead with half of the capital cities of the world on the bottom!

However, there is some real method to this sort of madness. Many large companies, as I said earlier, don't like (even have policies relating to this) working with sole traders, simply because they feel they need to know there is some kind of back-up available if things go wrong.

# Registering your company name and domain name

Don't forget that registering names is critical. For your company name, your accountant may be willing to do this on your behalf and that may be the simplest way. This will involve carrying out a full company search to check whether the name is available for use. The alternative, cheaper way is to do this yourself by going online at the Companies House website (www.companieshouse.gov.uk). There will be an initial fee to register your company, with an annual renewal fee, which are tax-deductible. This registration process at Companies House is for limited companies.

However, before you register a company name, you need to make sure that the equivalent domain name(s) (the one you will use in your e-mail address and web address) is available. This can be done by accessing online the many companies specialising in this area. To find them, use an Internet search engine and enter the phrase 'domain name registration'. The most popular domain names in the UK end with .com, .co.uk, .org, although there are others. Checking the availability of a domain name is free but there is a charge for registering the name(s). The charges vary, so shop around. Once you've paid the fee, your name is secure for one or two years and then there will be an annual renewal fee. If you find that someone else has already registered your preferred domain name, you might try contacting them to see if they would be willing to sell it to you.

## DON'T FOLLOW THIS EXAMPLE

I once knew a manager who had been terminated who spent the first week of his new career as an independent, creating a name for the company, designing a logo and then getting the whole caboodle of letterheads, envelopes, business cards, order forms, brochures and the like printed. Then he realised he wasn't any good at it and got another job. He never made a proposal, never even got a chance to ask for an order – but he did waste a lot of time on totally useless things.

My first lesson in this sort of corporate subterfuge came in 1982, my first year as an independent. I was asked to do some fairly intensive and confidential work for a major oil company. A consulting firm in New York who I was partnered with made it clear that my chances of getting any more business were minimal unless I changed my letterhead. So out went my beautiful letterhead with a italic script 'Mike Johnson' followed by 'Writer and Consultant'; in came 'Johnson & Associates Limited: Consultants in Corporate Communications'. On the letterhead was my name 'Michael A. Johnson' with the grand title 'Managing Partner' underneath.

Certainly I was still the same, but I had learned a lesson. If you want to appeal to corporations (large or small), you've got to make them feel comfortable with what you represent. It is a lesson I have never forgotten. Play their game, not yours. They want to believe (often very badly and urgently, because you are a solution) that you are part of them, so do it. It doesn't hurt at all, just makes you all the more professional (and most probably more expensive to hire).

Today, the line 'Consultants in Corporate Communication' has gone, replaced with 'Changing Corporate Perceptions', a phrase that opens up many avenues of activity.

### SORRY, I'VE GOT THE DECORATORS IN – AGAIN!

My very first 'office' was the spare bedroom of my apartment in Brussels. While carrying out a series of assignments for a large US multinational, there was a visiting senior vice-president, who kept wanting to come over and meet in my office. For six months the decorators were in residence, possibly the longest painting job in history! I got the message and quickly leased a second apartment in the same building as offices. Commuting a few floors to work each day and at last able to present a well-fitted out corporate front. *Advice*: If you can work close, but not 'at' home, do it. You'll save time, commuting costs and much frustration.

All this is about learning the 'Game'. The 'Game' is never played the way it looks when you are employed. But the Game is your day-to-day reality. What you have to be able to do is make your clients and prospective clients consider you as one of them. The more you 'fit' into their world, the happier they will be and the more business you'll get. It just makes the selling easier.

## Whose rules?

And to be considered as 'one of them', you have to learn their rules. Trouble is, if you have five or six clients, you need to learn five or six sets of rules and follow them. Not slavishly, but certainly enough to gain their respect. I wish I could begin to tell you how many corporate acronyms I have learned in 20-plus years. Why does every company and every industry have to have their own little codes for everything? Well they do – and if you want to succeed, you had better learn them and play their game. The rules – the only rules – are those that your clients play by. These are their touchstones, the things that make them feel comfortable and safe. Want to play in their sandbox? Then learn the sandbox rules.

One of the great things that has happened in recent years is that Microsoft has created a revolution by standardising much of what we now do. Yes, I know that Bill Gates is rich and that lots of people seem to dislike him for the monopoly he has created, but he has given us a basic standard for most of the systems we use (sorry Mac users, but you are able to communicate with us too). This has made a huge difference to most solo consultants, as before the majority of the world used Windows and its spin-offs, it was a nightmare trying to get anything to interface.

# Confidence is a keyword

Exuding confidence, even when things are going rapidly awry, is a key attribute of the successful independent consultant. Strangely enough, many clients will look to you when they are unsure of themselves. As an external adviser, you are often there to shore up their own lack of ability, vision or whatever. Never look confused, lost or out of your depth. As an old friend of mine once said, 'If you look poor, needy or desperate, you'll smell like a staked goat to a tiger.' Not a particularly nice allusion but right on the money! Clients can smell fear a mile away, and they don't like it any more than you do. They want to work with people who are confident, full of energy and ideas.

Having confidence is a critical part of the sell. Shrinking violets do not make great salespeople. But if you show that you know what you are doing, clients will welcome, even seek out, your counsel. They want to do business with people who make doing business easy. Never believe those stories that start out, 'I told my client just what he should do in no uncertain terms,' which in today's speak equates to: 'Dude, you're screwed!' Neither of these statements will help you sell. Anyone who suggests otherwise is wrong. The reason they have the time to tell you how clever they were is that they haven't got any business to keep them busy.

Clients also require your presence for two other – less well publicised – needs:

1 a shoulder to cry on
2 someone to blame.

Both of these happen – thankfully rather infrequently – and need to be taken into account. Crying clients are OK in small doses. Getting blamed is OK too as long as they don't have to fire you to make their point.

> **3** **TIP** If you've been out on the town and wake up with the mother of all hangovers, call in sick. It is the best – and hopefully ONLY – decision you'll make that day. Better to lose out on one or two days' fees than the whole business.

## Learn to ask for the business

Here I am repeating myself, but I can't underline the importance of this enough: you've got to learn to 'ask' for the business as a standard part of your routine. That act of asking is driven by confidence in your abilities. 'Of course they should give me the business, I'm good at this stuff,' is the attitude to take. If you avoid asking, they'll just think that you don't believe in yourself or your service enough to demand the business. They'll think you are not really worth the fee or perhaps, not ready for this level of assignment or responsibility.

Have I always got this right? No. Sometimes you don't want to be too pushy, sometimes a little voice in your head suggests that the time is not right. But all that comes with experience. As an old mentor of mine said, 'You should always ask, people can only say no.'

## Help your client to help himself

One early failing I have noticed in independents who are just starting out is a tendency to do the work they are given and nothing more. This is a big mistake. What you need to do – and many clients want and need this – is to develop a relationship where you are valued as much for your ideas as your delivery. For example, in my own case, my clients expect me to come up with marketing and business development ideas for their own businesses (sometimes to the detriment of my doing this for myself!).

As an outsider – by that I mean not an employee – you are in a unique position to give clients insights into opportunities they may otherwise miss. In my case, while working on a research project, I may well discover some alternative opportunities. Suggesting these to your client is taking care of them over and beyond the brief you have. Over the years I have become a *de facto* business developer and marketing executive for a host of firms who appreciate a different view on things.

The best idea is to formalise this arrangement. What you do is look at current projects you have and see how these could be developed or extended. Remember that you are doing this for the benefit of the client as much as for yourself. Get a reputation for adding value not just adding fees.

The same applies if you are in a general discussion. Make it clear what your overall talents are and be prepared to toot your horn a little. If you are working on your own, no one else will do it for you.

All this offers opportunities to play a greater role in your client's business. Just make sure you keep your independence and a balance of business. Remember, don't put all your beans in one tin.

# Intellectual property (IP)

Finally, a word about an issue that is growing in importance and is about the selling process in one way or another. You must make sure that you guard your intellectual property (IP). No matter how eager you are to close a deal, and the pressures on you to do that, make sure that you retain the ownership of your ideas (with consultants it is more likely to be ideas than anything else). For example, when you write an initial proposal, make it as brief as possible. Emphasise the advantages of doing the project without giving too much detail about the process. Especially don't give away contacts and ideas that others could use without involving you in the project.

Too often, I have seen consultants eager to get a piece of business, handing over the core ideas and plans for a project only to see it rejected by a prospective client, but then re-emerge at a later date without their involvement. Sure, there are a lot of really great people out there, sadly there are a small percentage that are pretty unscrupulous too. We'll get into more about IP in subsequent chapters. But let this act as a word of warning: guard your ideas very carefully, in the end they are all you have to offer.

# Key learning points

> If you can't sell, then you don't belong in the independent consulting game.

> You need to know how to 'ask for the order'.

> What to call your new business? Keep it simple and flexible: think of the future and don't box yourself in.

> Registering your chosen name is critical.

> Try to appear substantial. Big corporations like to work with people who appear to have back-up.

> Learn the clients' rules and play by them.

# Chapter **6**

# Marketing yourself

'If I had my life to live over again, I would elect to be a trader of goods rather than a student of science. I think barter is a noble thing.'

**Albert Einstein**

'Put all your eggs in one basket, and watch the basket.'

**Mark Twain**

Well, hopefully by now you are on your way. You've made a proposal, boldly asked for the order and been rewarded with some work. What you have done is to effectively 'sell' yourself. Congratulations! Now we need to move on and think about consolidating all that effort and moving into marketing mode. What this means for the independent consultant is putting yourself into a position where you get noticed – even sought out – by prospective clients. Is it really marketing? Well, yes and no. Frankly I think it is more personal public relations. You are creating a soft-sell platform for yourself. Remember always, in the career of an independent consultant, the product is YOU. How you do it may vary a great deal depending on what type of consulting you are involved in. So what we are going to do here is give you as many ideas as possible. Don't attempt to do all of this – you'll never get any client work done! Rather, pick and choose the types of marketing-related activity that are right for you.

The goal in all this is to get people to remember you, refer back to you and seek you out – this saves a great deal of time and is wonderful for anyone who doesn't really enjoy the thrill of the chase that is selling.

Let me illustrate this for you. For longer than I care to remember, I have had a note on my wall that is by now dog-eared and faded with age. But it is a little piece of advice that I have found worthwhile to refer to from time to time, as it puts into context what marketing for the independent is really all about. This is what the text says:

> If a boy meets a girl and he tells her how beautiful she is, how much he loves her and how he can't live without her – that's sales promotion.

> If a boy meets a girl and immediately impresses upon her how wonderful he is – that's advertising.

> But, if the girl seeks him out because she has heard from others what a fine chap he really is – that's public relations.

And that is what I think we independent consultants should aspire to in our self-marketing and business development. Our reputation is our best weapon for gaining business. The trick is how to enhance it.

Some people are born business developers. They seem to make it very effortless indeed. But in observing those types, I find that the so-called effortless image is based on a lot of hard work; and the harder you work, the easier it looks to outsiders. I have a work colleague who would get business if his plane crashed in the middle of the Amazon jungle or the Gobi desert. He is that good. He can smell a business opportunity 10 miles away. Most of us don't have that in-bred talent. So unless you are a business-generating dynamo, here are some thoughts and experiences that may help you on your way. These are not listed in any order of importance. Nor do I suggest you try and do them all. Just pick some of those that look like they'll work for you in your personal situation.

# Sales materials – how much, how soon?

Luckily for anyone entering the world of the independent consultant today, the technological revolution has made a lot of what us oldies needed to function in the past obsolete. More than that, the quality of office scanners, printers and copiers means that we can produce a great deal for ourselves (if we have the time and talent to do it).

How much you create and how you create it depends largely on the business you are in. Unless you really have a need to impress, or do mass sales campaigns, keep your money in your pocket and forget the glossy brochure – no one reads it. Don't forget that we live in a fast-moving, constantly changing world, so anything you commit to print has a rapidly diminishing shelf-life. It's far better to take what budget you have and invest it in a great website. That's my view – you don't have to do it this way.

> **TIP** Don't waste hours trying to create a desk-top brochure or presentation pack if you haven't got the skills to do it. Get an expert and pay them. You're a consultant – go consult!

I am a great believer in simplify, simplify, simplify, especially when it comes to spending money on things you may not really need. Here's the Mike Johnson minimalist starter kit (although time will tell if you need to modify this for your business). And, for good measure, I've given you some advice on each item. This might seem obvious to you, but I never cease to be surprised what people come up with, especially these days where technology has allowed us to be 'do-it-yourself' designers. Please, let the professionals do some of this for you, or at the very least the main things that matter. In a techno-driven world what follows might seem ridiculously basic – it isn't. It's showing off who you are in the best way possible.

## Business cards

Now, surely there can't be much complicated about a business card? Want to bet on that? A business card is not just a little piece of paper, it is a hard-copy tool that says a great deal about you and your business. Get it wrong, send the wrong message, and there is a little piece of you (a wrong piece of you) forever filed in someone's Rolodex. Here are some things about business cards you need to know.

> Make the card the very best quality you can. Why? It needs to stay rigid in your pocket, attached to a letter, and in the sticky, sweaty hand of the person you have given it to. It also needs to feel crisp and solid on contact – just like you!

> Make the important details clearly readable. Don't have print so small, over-designed or in pastel shades that people can't read it.

> If you must print on two sides, to squeeze in lots of irrelevant stuff about yourself, make sure that the contact details are on ONE SIDE ONLY.

> Try, try, try (and this applies to any other print as well) to create a logo that has a single colour; it saves on print costs and on print cartridge costs too. Then use a simple black ink for the information – it copies well.

> Don't fill the card with irrelevant detail. Let it tell who you are, what you do and where you operate from.

> Business cards should be horizontal, not vertical. If you must succumb to some graphic designer's creativity, try and make sure that he keeps the information easy to read. Often information – like phone and e-mail data – is viewed as a nuisance to creative types!

> Maximum size of a functional business card is 85mm x 55mm. Any bigger and it won't fit into a pocket, a standard business card wallet, a Rolodex (yes, we smart people still use them) and countless other places where they should (luggage tags, portable scanners, free meal competition boxes in restaurants, etc.).

> No photographs of yourself – ever, under any circumstances – on either the front or the back.

## Letterheads

Like the business card, your letterhead says a great deal about you. Why then do so many people not get it right? A letterhead is a lot more than a single sheet of paper with your logo and trading details on. It is a multi-use document and should be carefully developed. Again it is part of the image you want to create. Here are some things about letterheads you may need to know:

> Like your business card, use the very best paper you can. Something with a bit of 'feel' to it. And make sure it is a decent weight – 120g is ideal. Don't try and do it on the kind of paper you use for cheap print-outs or copying (around 80g), it doesn't set the tone you want.

> Consider a light coloured paper – grey, cream. It can 'lift' your image – as long as it doesn't clash with your logo.

> Get the company name (and logo) printed at the top in the colour(s) you require, but add all the rest of the details (address, phones, bank, registration etc.) yourself. These details can change. This way you stay flexible and save money too.

> Print the name and logo at the top (horizontal and centred). Then you can use it as a second and subsequent sheet, adapt it for reports and proposals, cover notes and so on. Fancy designs end up costing you fancy money. So, logos that are vertical or tucked in corners might seem like a cool move, but they just turn out to be inflexible impositions on what you can do.

## Envelopes

Yes, there are even things to learn about envelopes – unless you want to have a stock of unused ones cluttering up your limited work space.

> Buy white ones. Don't waste money on expensive envelopes, only geeks and the mailroom clerk examine envelopes.

> Buy various standard sizes: for letters (80g, no window) 220mm x 110mm: For invoicing, same as above but with a window. For larger packages (115g) 381mm x 254mm, and something similar with padding to protect documents.

> I either print out envelopes myself, or use labels with name and address on and an ink stamp for bulky packages. Envelopes with your logo and name on seem an unnecessary expense, particularly in start-up stage.

> I also have a stock of CD mailer envelopes, which I find useful for all sorts of lightweight items, not just CDs.

## Compliment slips

I find that these have multiple uses and are a great investment for any independent. I carry a stock with me wherever I go.

> Again use that 120g paper, the same as your letterhead. Sizes can vary from A5 to A6, depending on your needs.

> Attach them to documents, as they can be simply hand-written (adding to the personal touch).

> Use them as quick thank-you notes, again personalising a contact.

> Use them as memo pads, your printer can make them up that way.

> Use them as 'spare paper' and give them to other people. Those that can never find anything to write on!

Then all you need is the best website your money can buy (see next item).

**PRINT YOUR WAY TO OBLIVION**

Here's a lesson. I had a friend who was made redundant from his high-powered job as a very senior human resources professional. He was generously compensated. His dream had always been to work as an independent in creating new learning environments for employees. Using his redundancy pay-out, he created a business which initially met with some small success. Encouraged, he began to produce marketing and sales material of incredible quality. It was so good, when I first saw it I thought this was from a big consulting firm. A book (which he paid to be published) followed, plus position papers and reports – all with the same high production values (and consequent high costs). Then one day, there was no money coming in, and the materials he had so carefully crafted (when he should have been out selling) were getting out of date. He is now back in the corporate world again. What he failed to see was that he had created too much of a good thing. Too glossy, too soon, taking too much time from what should have been his main focus – getting out, meeting people, building a basic business.

# The website

For virtually all independents, your website is THE marketing tool of today. Forget brochures and other print, spend your money on a website that does you proud. I make no apologies here, I am going to keep hammering on about this no brochure thing. You don't need them until you are rich and then they are just an ego-trip. To my mind, the website is the electronic version of the corporate brochure anyway. The beauty of it is that it doesn't cost thousands to change and fix.

Here are my tips about websites that you may find useful:

> Even if you are technically savvy, get someone else involved. Why waste your time doing this when you could be running your business? Preferably find someone nearby, who you can easily go round and see face-to-face. Check them out with others and see just how good they are. The best way to get a website helper is to see who gets recommended in your business or in your geographic area.

> Make sure it's YOU and not the website designer that has all the access codes or at least a way to get at them easily. Website creators are often transient, or not very good at staying in business. You need to be in control.

➤ Register your URL in as many ways as you can. The web isn't going away and the more bits you own, the more flexible you can be both now and in the future.

➤ If you plan to diversify, register a domain name as soon as you can too. As we said earlier, so many people are seeking the right 'address' that it is getting more difficult. Get as many as you can (.com .org .uk (or your country of operation) .eu) and so on.

➤ Make sure your designer isn't some madman with a Mac and little else in the technique department. We are in business here, not trying to imitate Andy Warhol. An over-designed website is like an over-designed business card, it says a lot about you – most of it not useful or conducive to bringing in business.

➤ Visit frequently your chosen 'webmaster' and then plan your update material so as to keep down costs. Remember, every time they touch that keyboard it is like a taxi-meter, click, click, click. Go and visit them when you have a series of things to do, it costs a great deal less. Every 4 to 8 weeks would seem fine, unless you have a lot of activity to report on.

➤ Keep it simple, simple, simple. Especially on the Home Page, less is more.

➤ Think long and hard about what your website is supposed to do. For most independent consultants it is a shop window, displaying their talents and skills and offering services. But maybe you need more than that. If you are selling products online you will need a much more complex set-up and possibly more technical assistance.

# The electronic calling card *par excellence*

A website is your showroom. In fact it is a lot more than that. It not only shows what you can do, it vouches for you. It is a 365 days-a-year testimonial. Time after time I am on the phone trying to agree meetings, set up interviews and so on, and the person I am calling will say, 'Yes, I'm on your website, I see who you are now.' This is a security system in a way. There is no good trying to bluff your way into a company any more. Today people ask, 'What's your site?' And you can't say, 'well I don't have one.' Everyone has one (my neighbour's dog has one for goodness sake!). I'm an oldie in this independent consulting business and I have to tell you that this is the best thing that ever happened to us as a group of professionals.

Reason? I can do things I could never do before. I can work in places and with people as never before. I may have been able to do it in theory, but I couldn't in practice because time (travel) and money (cost of getting to places) put a great barrier in the way. The 'E' revolution has changed all that. In the past 12 months I have completed projects in the US, Sweden and Switzerland without ever setting foot in any of those places. The only reason I could do those projects was the availability of the 'E' world to help me. Opportunity is at the end of our fingertips. You just need a big bag of creativity to make it happen.

2 **TIP** What your website does is give you instant credibility: something that could take years (and a huge budget) to establish before this great invention. This is possibly the most significant aid to the independent consultant ever devised – use it.

## Learn to link

An effective website is a magical link to the outside world for any independent consultant. It can offer ever more opportunities to extend your credibility through linking to other sites that underscore your excellence as a consultant. Publish an article (see later) and it not only goes on your website, it's on the publisher's site too. Agree to speak at a conference and your presentation – even you live – can be featured on the event's pre and post report sites as well. Create links with other – supportive – consultants and you have the basis of a powerful online network.

Whatever you do, don't underestimate the power of today's technology. But don't fall into the trap of thinking that it can solve all your problems – it can't. Clients still expect the consultants they employ and work with to be and look professional. And that begins with those basics I have described above. Get those right and you have built a foundation for your ongoing business development. And it has been done at very little cost.

## The art of cold calling – don't

All of us hate making cold calls (if you are the weird exception, please contact me). But, of course, if we hear that there may be some opportunities emerging in an organisation, we know we need to follow this up. Problem is, most cold calls just don't work. What you need is some way to turn a cold call into something else: if not a hot call, then at least a warm sort of call. A way to get you from feeling like a telesales person into what you really are: a very smart consultant, whom they need. Well, you can do it. What it takes is a bit of work and planning – but it can happen.

The very best 'new business' call you can make is one of those, 'Jim asked me to call you' sort. The prospect knows and admires Jim, so you are recommended. You get work. Sadly, those 'Jim asked me to call' routines are few and far between for many of us. So how do you get that all important foot in the door?

If you are going to turn your back on cold calls, you need an effective substitute. And I have the answer. At the risk of unleashing thousands of independent consultants around the world feverishly calling punters, here's the way to do it:

YOU NEED A LEGITIMATE REASON TO CALL

Yes, yes, yes. I can hear you saying it now, 'Oh, that's clever!, did I just spend real money on a real book to get to Chapter 6 and be told that?' Well, yes you did. And now I am going to tell you how to do it.

What you are required to do is to be able to engage someone in a conversation. That is all you need, a reason, excuse to talk. This is not about faking stuff, this is not about, 'our consultants are currently on the prowl in your area.' This is about creating real, meaningful, content-rich conversations.

You see you don't – in fact you must never – sell anything. All you are going to do is pander to someone's curiosity and flatter their ego a little. Strangely enough, everyone likes that.

The 'legitimate' reason to call (the excuse) has to be just that, REAL. Well it has to be real when I do it, because I am not very good at stretching truths. What I created some time ago was the research-led enquiry line. Basically, what you do is devise a piece of business-related research (which you will publish) and use that as your door opener.

As you can imagine, this works much better if you are carrying out research for some easily recognisable organisation or institution. So, one of the best ways to make this work really well is to get into bed with an organisation or institution (on a no-fee basis if necessary) and volunteer your services.

In my own case I have been pretty lucky, because I have become associated with a lot of research initiatives over the years, so I have already achieved a certain level of credibility. I have also published a lot (and have the evidence on my website to prove it).

But my suggestion to you is to start small and work your way up. For example, if you are working in a small community, develop and then create a study for your local chamber of commerce or similar group. This will allow you to visit members – and others in the business community – at their places of work. At the end of the study you self-publish (if necessary) and then organise a seminar or workshop on the findings. You can do this at any level – local, national, international, it is all the same in the end – all you need is the great idea that will catch people's interest.

I have even developed a version of this research-led business development approach for clients who were seeking to expand their business horizons. What we did was link up with a publisher and then carry out and publish a series of research papers: launching them with a road-show of seminars. Most times, when you call a 'target', they are only too happy to oblige. The total legitimacy of the action comes, of course, at the end when you send them a copy of the report or book you have completed. The plan then is that this will lead to follow-up enquiries and opportunities to discuss your research with them at a suitably senior level.

## Get yourself published

Getting around to writing a book that reinforces your professional expertise is another way of getting to meet new business prospects. In all these cases you end up with a hard-copy report or similar which becomes your current 'brochure'. And it will sell you a lot better than any glossy piece you can come up with yourself. By getting published, you are being legitimised by others. That is a very powerful statement, and one that prospects can't argue with.

## Excuses to stay in touch

Of course, you can't always be writing a book or researching some emerging business issue (people will wonder if you ever do any real work!). So other reasons to stay in contact with those prospective clients you met have to be created. In this, I find that a newsletter, short on sell and big on content, works very well indeed. But it only works well when it begins to appear on a regular basis (my view is that it takes four issues before anyone comes to accept anything that drops onto their desk). Newsletters are not expensive to produce and print (less than a brochure) and creating four issues a year is a sort of minimum. I would emphasise that regularity, it really is important. And so is the content. Don't sell, TELL. Most clients you'll find are so busy fighting their own fires that anyone who gives them some tips and insights will be really appreciated.

The type that I produce are in hard-copy and an electronic version, but it is the hard-copy that gets read by clients and prospects (usually at home, on a train or in a plane). Content is geared closely to their interests and is designed to provide a topical commentary on issues related to (in my case) communications, human resources, and the office of the future. In my experience, newsletters more than pay for themselves. They give you some immediate recognition, but also act as a permanent reminder that you are always available to solve the problems you are warning them about.

> **TIP** The other great thing about newsletters with a rich content is that you can use them as intellectual input for your website – again creating some professional gravitas.

## Hot-topic seminars

Another way of staying in touch is to organise and run seminars or work-shops on hot topics that you know will appeal to your prospective audience. These days the competition to mount these sort of events is increasing, so it isn't easy to get a good turnout, unless the subject is really compelling. All the same, it is worth trying to make this happen as you have a captive audience (who always appreciate NOT being sold to). Remember, know from the outset what you want to achieve. Don't invite too many people. If you are on your own, six or seven is the maximum so you get a lot of interaction and a lot of opportunity to talk with the audience. Neither the setting nor the hospitality needs to be lavish – just appropriate. Remember, it is your professionalism they will be checking up on – not the quality of the catering.

## Platform marketing: conferences and seminars

Getting invited to speak at conferences and seminars is another way to get your ideas and your business offering across. But make sure that you are going to generate the right amount of publicity for yourself and your services. Too many conference organisers seek to limit the commercial exposure you can have. If that is the case, it may not be worth actually doing the session. Also, carefully check out the reputation of the organisers and make certain they are a legitimate operator – not all of them are. As I said earlier in the book, don't agree to speak at a conference or seminar for free, unless you know you'll get some business out of it. Good professionals don't need unfocused network opportunities. All too often the promised opportunity to meet with delegates doesn't work out. Ask for a fee and expenses. If they don't want to pay, politely decline.

A few points to keep in mind here:

> Unless there is a guarantee of paid work coming from the session, say no.

> 'This is a great networking opportunity for you Mr Johnson' translates as, 'we haven't got any budget to pay you.' Or even the far more insulting, 'all the other, really important people said "no".' Why you would want to spend a large chunk of your billable time talking for free to a group of people who are all getting paid their salaries to be there?

> Remember, it is NEVER just a day out of your time. Preparation and travel time mean two or three days in total.

> Check out what the organisers are going to say about you. Make sure you get what you want.

> Insist on a full briefing. Who are the audience; how big is it; what do they expect from the session? Is it a presentation (for how long) or is there question time too? Most important, are there any other sessions they want you involved in?

> Make sure you can distribute contact details, reports, newsletters and so forth. There's not much point in being there if you can't advertise.

And one last piece of advice. Make sure you book your own travel. That keeps your arrangements as flexible as they need to be. Often speaking assignments are planned months ahead and you don't know what you will be doing nearer that date, do you?

## Samples and show reels

As I mentioned earlier, samples are great. The reason I write books is for the marketing value, not the sales. The reason I research and produce investigative reports is to gain access to new opportunities. So, make sure you do a deal to get free or deeply discounted copies of any work from the publisher before you sign the contract.

In addition, if you get an opportunity to be filmed during a presentation, make sure you get a copy of the CD with permission to use it. The same with radio interviews. Then you can either use them as discreet mailers or put them on your website. If you are attending a conference that is being recorded, ensure you get a copy of the film or audio tape afterwards, again on CD.

# Creating your own network

We covered a lot about networks in Chapter 2, suggesting that it isn't a very wise move to start working for yourself if you don't have some kind of effective network in place. The other option – especially once you are an established 'name' – is to create your own network. To give you an idea of how this can be done, let me explain how I created the FutureWork Forum (a group of like-minded, but non-competing independent consultants). Check it out on www.futureworkforum.com.

My initial plan was to have an information exchange between people I knew and respected who were in the same position as myself. It was – in the early days – a security blanket made up of people I could talk to and check out ideas with. You may recall we covered this in Chapter 2, where we talked about needing shoulders to cry on. FutureWork Forum was my personal, professional shoulder, not really for crying onto, but for bouncing ideas off.

After we had met a few times face-to-face, I – and the rest in the group – began to realise the collective power and experience we had. Its depth of knowledge, time in the market, and eagerness to stay up to date were incredible. Indeed, we had not just a 'talking' shop but the foundations of a 'doing' organisation. And while everyone was their own boss, there was an increasing sense of collective belief and understanding. On that basis, I and the other members (we are 18 individuals) are now very much a part of the FutureWork Forum. We run workshops in cities all over Europe and beyond. We carry out research and write about the future world of work.

But there are spin-offs. And these are the real advantages to creating and maintaining a network. When I go to present to a client or a prospect, I carry 17 other people with me on my shoulder. All 17 are eager and available to help. When my clients ask 'Where is your support?', I say it is everywhere and it is across the whole gamut of human issues in business. I am still a sole trader, but I am also so much bigger than that. My business proposition, my consulting expertise is hugely enhanced by the presence of 17 other professionals – all with great track records in their specialist fields.

Suffice to say, having a network that is strong but non-invasive (which still lets me do my job the way I want to) has improved my ability to market myself (proving that even after 20 years there is still a lot to learn) and to better meet my clients' emerging needs. Moreover, it places me – a solo independent consultant – as a true global player, who can call on advice, ideas and influence from around the world and bring that expertise back to my clients.

## If you can't do it – teach it!

I have never believed that phrase above. What I do believe is that we can as independents make a huge contribution by passing on our knowledge and experience to others. We can give a lot of our expertise and our time to help educate the next generation. Again, do this and your personal stock and recognition level will increase. You'll also – unless you are a complete dunce –get a great deal of personal satisfaction out of it. You don't have to think of it as a part of the marketing process if you don't want to. Just know that it is. For independents, everything you do is part of marketing yourself, even if you don't recognise or treat it as such.

## Charitable work

Into that list comes charitable work. If you can teach, coach, add up numbers or help to sell things, you are wanted somewhere, somehow. Many of us in our early years of struggle to establish ourselves have little time for this. But again, as I said above, this too is a type of marketing. In charitable work I have been involved in I have met two good clients. Two people I would possibly never have come across if I had not been giving my time. Indeed, that opportunity for sole traders can appear at any time and in any place. It is getting to recognise that opportunity and act on it that is the mark of the true independent professional.

## Gifts to go

Finally, a silly subject to end this chapter with – gifts. Someone asked me, 'What do you do about gifts to your clients and prospects?' Answer?

Nothing. I cannot see that pens, miniature radios, talking calendars and so on have anything to do with my business, my ability to get more, or my ability to deliver what my clients want and expect. Sure, I take my clients out to dinner from time to time, but basically it's all down to making sure you do a good job – that, I believe, is what clients really appreciate and expect. Oh, and I'll send them a copy of my latest book or research report, which I would like to think adds to their education. Of course, there are some people who see giving as an intrinsic part of how they do business. It isn't for me and I don't see that it has any real place in the marketing of professional services. Most likely my clients would hint at the fact I was getting too successful and making too much money!

Don't forget in all this that you are marketing yourself. You ARE the product. That is what the client buys, at least for now. So, at present, the only person you can let down is yourself.

## THINKING INSIDE THE BOX

I have a pal of mine who is a civil engineering consultant. While that may sound grand, my pal has always played it very low-key. There are no glorious suspension bridges or motorways in his body of work, but there are a lot of cycle tracks, woodland walks, public toilets (including those special areas for dogs) and children's play areas. He is largely an unsung professional, going about his work quietly and without any fuss. While others seek stardom and reputation enhancement, he is happy with a 20-mile fence to plan.

One day I asked him, 'How do you market yourself?'

'Well I don't suppose I do,' he replied. 'Never thought about it.'
'Well how do you get your business?' I said. 'Do you apply for tenders and stuff like that?', knowing that most of his work was in the local public sector.
'Oh no, I don't do that. Well I don't need to. The hampers seem to take care of it.'
'What hampers?' I asked.
'The ones that I give to the ladies who schedule the work at the council offices,' he said. 'You see I used to buy them from the Harrods' catalogue, but they got really expensive. So now I just buy 20 large wicker hampers and fill them myself.'
My mate ensures that each year the ladies who get the work distributed after it has been agreed by the local council get a hamper (after

▶

◄ more than 10 years they expect them). There are NO favours. All that happens is that the work assigned to my pal, somehow, miraculously rises through the order pile to the very top. Now that's marketing!

## Dressing for success

So, you're an independent consultant. How do you dress? Are there any rules these days that need to be followed? As far as I am concerned, there is only one. Dress to show that you respect your client and his or her environment. If you want a second rule: When in doubt, overdress, you can always take something off!

Let me explain this a little. Twenty years ago, life was pretty easy in the sartorial stakes. If you were a man, you wore a suit and tie and that was that. If you were in a serious profession that suit was probably dark; if you were in a more liberal profession you might have run to light grey. Today things are different.

My clients vary by industry, geography and size. They all have their dress codes and sub-dress codes. However, my rule is number one above: Dress to show that you respect your client and his or her environment. By that I mean, if I am going into a good, solid professional firm where everyone wears suits and ties, I will too. If I am going into a new media environment, where everyone wears jeans and t-shirts I won't wear that (at my age I'd look ridiculous!), but I won't wear the tie.

This rule is, of course, equally applicable to women, who need to look smart and professional in the working environment. Remember to respect local customs too; particularly if it's a Muslim country, try to dress modestly. But in addition to a smart buisness suit, remember to take along something dressier for the evenings.

## Key learning points

> Get the basic things right from the outset: business cards, letterheads – they are the 'anchors' of your business.

> Make your website your showroom.

> Find excuses for making calls, never be forced into a completely cold call – they seldom work and make you look desperate.

> Create your own network, but remember it is variety you need – not people in the same business as you.

> Use seminars and conferences as a showcase, but stay in control.

> Be careful how you dress: keep it simple and smart.

# Chapter **7**

## New business

### Getting it, charging for it, getting paid for it

*'Being in your own business is working 80 hours a week so that you can avoid working 40 hours a week for someone else.'*

**Ramona Arnett**

*Business? That's very simple – it's other people's money.*

**Alexander Dumas**

# Creating your new business policy

When the phone rings or the e-mail pings and you are asked to make a proposal, know what your game-plan is. If you are really new to all this, you'll be dancing around the room and have already spent the mega-mounds of money you are about to make. Then reality strikes and you begin to wonder what is the best way forward. If you are really new to this stuff then you do need to consider carefully where you fit into all of this. There are some basic rules that never change over time, no matter how big, how successful and how broad your business offering gets. If you cannot generate new business, you cannot sustain yourself. Being an independent consultant (an independent anything come to that) is about surviving. It's like nature. After winter comes spring (but did you plant those seeds?); then summer, when you bask in all the great things you created. Then, of course, the cold winds of autumn, when you need to ensure there are good things (it's called money) in your storehouse, for the winter that will arrive. In business, the seasons don't follow a 12-month cycle (on bad days they can all appear within 24 hours!). So, be careful, be frugal. Be bold too! And that final thing. Remember paranoia? Yes, be paranoid too. Forty-nine per cent of the time that works. Only paranoid people believe that, of course!

Based on 25 years of heartache and pain, here are my rules for generating business.

## Rules for generating business

**New business rule 1:** Always give a first meeting at no charge and then keep that time sheet and build all the other pre-assignment meets into your budget (remember this is your budget that YOU see, not the one you show the client). If the business doesn't come after meeting three, it probably won't. Then again ...

*Paranoid business rule 1*: You've had those three meetings and nothing. But maybe it will all work out – won't it? Shouldn't I keep trying just once more? And then perhaps one more time after that? The answer to that is, I really don't know. If you are very busy, move on. If you are eating brown rice and drinking tap water, go on, have another go. By that time no one will care except you.

**New business rule 2:** Never give away the farm. Unless you know the people very well, never make a detailed proposal the first time. I've done it, so has everyone else. In my case they took it, loved it and shut the door in my face. Months later I saw it being implemented by another consulting firm. It was a hard lesson learned. Now I give a broad outline and some likely costs to get the discussion moving. And I always leave some things out (and definitely any contacts or names of other people I would use). If anyone objects, then the line is: 'Well I know you are busy, and I didn't want to bog you down in detail until we agree the basics'. This always works for me. Then again ...

*Paranoid business rule 2*: You may be tempted to give them just a bit of your hard-earned knowledge. Don't! If they are really professional they won't ask that. And for certain people, be really, really paranoid and never let them know anything about your secrets, your contacts, your ways of working. Why? Because they'll steal them. Not out of any real nastiness, but because it is just second nature to them – that's what they do.

**New business rule 3:** If it looks too good to be true – then it IS too good to be true! Keep your feet planted firmly on the ground. Consider the client; what do they look like, what do they represent? Check them out. Don't take anything at face value. Think, 'Do I really want to do business with these people?' Then phone a friend for advice. Then again ...

*Paranoid business rule 3*: Being as paranoid as above is quite sufficient. You see, you are learning.

**New business rule 4:** Show me the money! In any new business venture, invoice one-third up-front (plus that 10-15 per cent expense advance). If they are serious, they will pay it. Don't commit until you get that. This will do two things: (a) earn their respect and (b) make sure you don't end up hiring debt collectors. If they want what you have got to sell, they will pay. Then again ...

*Paranoid business rule 4*: It doesn't always work like this. Usually, people when they finally get around to saying 'yes' want the damn thing done yester-day. If every independent consultant waited until the paperwork and the money arrived, we'd all be out of business. The best thing to do is to make sure (feel it in your guts, more like) that you are dealing with straight people.

**New business rule 5:** Share your good news and get a contract. Pieces of paper (signed by both parties) are useful. Get a deal signed and sealed and file it with your lawyer. Again, if they really want you, that won't be a problem either. Then again ...

*Paranoid business rule 5*: Yes, it can take time. And if you don't get started, they'll think you don't want to work for them. Once again, it's your call, your judgement.

Once you've done this a few times, you'll know what is good and what is bad. You'll be able to read the signs like a gypsy fortune-teller. It's a pity crystal balls aren't for real. We could really use them – you could even build a consulting business on them.

## Writing proposals that work

My somewhat cynical view is that few proposals ever get read in any great detail. Pressed-for-time executives probably read the opening creative bit and then turn to the costs. But there are – to my mind – several simple rules about getting proposals in front of prospective clients that give you a better-than-even chance of it getting read and agreed, and therefore you getting work.

**Writing proposals rule 1: Make it original.** Too often I see proposals that have been tarted up from some standard example in a Microsoft Word file. While I may refer back to previous proposals, I always write each new one afresh. That way they seem to just fit with a client's needs better and seem just that – fresher. It takes time to do, but I believe (I have no hard evidence for this) it delivers a higher strike rate in winning business.

**Writing proposals rule 2: Make it short.** As I said earlier, don't give away your secrets, but also keep it nice and short (you can send a longer specification-ridden version if you get the business or it becomes necessary in protracted negotiations) so that you get their attention.

**Writing proposals rule 3: Make it formal.** Send an e-version by all means, but also send a hard-copy version. It looks professional and shows a certain amount of respect for the prospective client and for the project you are bidding on. Call me old-fashioned, but I send a hard-copy (snail-mail) for quite a few things. Serious memos, project plans and so on get an e-mail for speed and a hard-copy by post as a back-up. I have countless examples where the e-mail never got read in the clutter of an electronic in-box, but the snail-mail did!

**Writing proposals rule 4: The 24-hour delay tactic**. No matter how urgent, try to give yourself 24 hours to reflect on your proposal before you send it out. Close the office, come back the following morning and reread it. I am certain you will change at least one significant item (usually that cheap budget line to try and keep initial costs down).

**Writing proposals rule 5: Check it out!** So many proposals I see have really bad spelling errors and other faults. Make sure it not only looks good but is good. Get someone else to read it at least twice. Again, I guarantee you'll make corrections: that 24-hour rule again.

> **TIP**: The 24-hour delay tactic also works when you are really angry about something. Don't fire off that smart-assed reply – you'll regret it come morning. Sit on it for 24 hours and things will look a whole lot different.

# When to chase for the business

There should be a seminar on this subject. I have never met anyone, anywhere in any business who knows the real answer to when to call up and ask. Indeed, I have two good friends and every time we meet we discuss the psychology of when to call the prospective client. Call too soon and you look too eager. Call too late and they think (wrongly, of course) that you didn't want the business badly enough. Call on the wrong day and that's trouble too. My view has come down to this: when YOU think it is time to call, it probably is. I have agonised over this for so long that I am now considering just letting it run for 72 hours and following up, regardless of who it is or the type of assignment I am bidding on.

The trouble is that we begin to play mind-games with ourselves (there's that old paranoia kicking in again). We think that our prospective client is ignoring us. The reality is that there are a thousand-and-one other things on his or her desk that demand attention. What is our big issue is a drop in the ocean to them. So we sit and fret or sulk and wonder. And what we wonder about is never anything to do with reality. Of course it isn't – we're paranoid after all!

So my advice is send in your proposal and then after 72 hours, make that call. That gives you an acceptable gap not to look too eager, but just enough time to seem concerned that you get the business. Am I right? Frankly I haven't got a clue! On this one you are really on your own. But if you ever hear of a seminar on this or come up with a definitive answer, let me know.

## Making the PA your pal

One way of upping your chances of getting in front of your prospective client is to schmooze the personal assistant. I spend a lot of time on that. Consequently, I rarely call my most senior contacts (they are never in their offices anyway), just phone their PAs and have chats about how busy their boss is and stuff like that. Then you say, 'I'd like to get the chance of a meet' and you get to the top of the list very quickly indeed.

Lots of people don't believe this. But I have found it to work for me time and time again. There is another thing that really does get ignored. If your client moves on, they rarely take their PA with them (especially if they leave the organisation). This is a really great opportunity if you have set it up right. I can't begin to add up the business I have got by my former client's PA introducing me to the new incumbent in the job. So treat the PAs with respect and be nice to them. Make them your friend. Many people treat PAs badly face-to-face and on the phone. It's like dealing with the check-in clerk at the airport – the nicer you are, the better seat you get.

## Setting fees and other money worries

Setting a realistic fee level isn't easy for the first timer. What you charge is determined so much by the business you are going to be conducting, the type of clients you will have, and where you will be doing this. A young accountant starting out on his or her own in Cornwall is going to be charging very differently from a middle-aged, highly experienced accountant in London who wants to try their hand at going it alone. Similarly, a training consultant in the Midlands working mainly for the public sector is going to set fees differently to a personal coach for the director of a FTSE listed company in London.

The very best way to begin to understand what to charge is to ask. Yes, there's a lot of asking in this business! If you don't know anyone operating in your chosen independent profession, find someone. The easiest way to do this is to embark on some market research. Google your area or pick up the local Yellow Pages, trade directories or local chamber of commerce handbooks (all available at your local library and most probably online) and make up a list of likely targets. Then call them and ask about their fees on the excuse that you want to consider hiring them. This is NOT a crime! Chances are, you'll get some great ideas and also get an indication of what extras they charge and why. And it can pay off even better than that. I know of several independent consultants who just by researching what the competition was doing found out that they had a skills shortage and got immediate, lucrative work from them. As an independent, never forget that opportunity lies around every corner.

Once you begin to understand the local market, you can set your fees accordingly. And that comes from knowing what you have to offer against what is already available in the marketplace.

> **2** **TIP** Remember, the 'local' market is the one you play in. If you are highly specialised, your local market can cover the globe. I know a guitar consultant, who travels the world for rich clients. He has two 'competitors' that he knows of, but their fees are remarkably similar and one is in Japan and one in California. Your 'local' business is peculiar to you and those that also undertake it. Similarly, an independent specialised trainer will have 'local' competition, but only for people who require his services.

First know the market you are going to play in. By understanding it intimately, you can make a clear-cut decision about what you are going to do. If you are seeking volume, you might try undercutting the competition in your 'local' market. If you want to go for a high price, know why you are doing that. However, remember one thing – once you drop your price it isn't easy to put it up again.

Yes, we've all been there. When business gets lousy, as it does from time to time, you will come under pressure to drop prices. Clients and prospective clients will tell you that your competitors have lowered prices by 25 per cent or even more. This poses a test of your confidence and also your business ability. Seldom are things as they seem. If you are going to stay in business, you may agree to take on some short-term assignments at a lower overall fee to keep your operations running.

If you do face this dilemma, protect your hourly or daily fee base by offering a project price. That way your usual fees never get called into question. But never get into long-term, fee-based commitments that way. Similarly, anyone who says that they have never cut their prices is definitely not telling the truth. What you need to do is to limit the damage. Make sure this is seen very much as a favour to your client, but make sure that they value and understand that decision (call it a sacrifice, if you must!). Also get them back to the original fees as quickly as you can. If you have gone onto a project-based structure, you can crank these up quite easily, without giving them any cause for alarm.

Sometimes (let's say 'always', and be honest!) in really good economic times prices do mushroom. Usually clients are happy to pay increasing consulting fees, because they are making good money too. So certainly there are times when fees do need a bit of correction, when we all get too fat and sassy. But everyone knows that they will creep back up as soon as economic growth sets in again. A kind of symbiotic relationship develops. When the good times roll, you roll with them and learn to do that and build some fat for the bad days ahead. When those bad days arrive, most clients want you to join them in the pain process. Looking fit and prosperous while your clients are on an extreme diet is not good.

3 **TIP** When times are bad for your clients, never turn up at their premises in a flash new car – it's professional suicide.

## THE TIME BENDERS

Time is a peculiar thing – you can even stretch it to make money. Here's how to do it. Some years ago, I had a new competitor in town. Very aggressive and very much selling on price: a price seriously undercutting my own. After a few months, I was bidding on a piece of work and lost out. I asked – always ask, people can only say 'no' – why we lost. 'Here's why', said my contact and she threw my rival's proposal (not really an ethical thing to do) across the desk at me. I looked at it. His hourly fees were almost half of mine! What they had done was buy on price. But they didn't really do that at all. They were mesmerised by the idea of a very low hourly fee (so was I!). There was no way anyone could make money like this. Then I looked at the rest of the document. Essentially, total fees for the project from my competitor and myself were the same. The only difference was that he was – when you examined the proposal closely – going to take a lot more time to do it.

Here's how it works.

If I bid £100/hour (using a six-hour chargeable day as a guide) that's £600/day
If the project is estimated to take 5 days, that's £3,000.
If my competitor bids at £60/hour, that's £360.
But if he then takes twice as long to complete it, that's 10 days and £3,600.

Is that clever? No. That isn't the clever part. What you actually do (without telling the client, of course) is to complete the project in five days and bill them for 10. But, you say, they are claiming it will take them longer. Yes, they do, but the real visible part of the pitch is the hourly and the daily fees.

# The variable fee game

Unless you are purely in this independent existence for the money alone (in which case, go take a high-paid job somewhere instead), there are times when dropping your fees (so that only YOU know that) makes really good sense. Assuming that a large part of your decision to go into business for yourself was prompted by the fact that you like what you do and have quite a passion for it, creating variable fee structures (for all sorts of reasons) makes a good deal of sense.

Indeed, variable fee structures are something that few other consultants (and certainly the medium and large ones) can manage (usually because they have a lot of hungry junior consultants to feed and the system can't take this sort of serendipitous flexibility), so once again it gives us real independents a true competitive edge.

My own version of variable fees is based on a lot of experience gained over the years. While I will charge a full rate for my services to anyone who is clearly able to pay, I'll come and go quite a lot for something that I really want to do because it will (a) do my own reputation a lot of good and (b) help with other projects I am involved in. Likewise, I will do pro bono work on the basis that, yes, of course, it helps others, but it also widens my network, adds to my own knowledge, and so on. One of the greatest thing that independents have is just that – their independence. You are master of your own universe. Don't forget that. All of us do at some time or another and need to be reminded of it regularly.

# Marking-up work

If you use other independents to help you out, should you mark up their work when you bill the client? Frankly, I think it really is up to the individual and the circumstances. Over many years I have used other consultants, commercial artists, photographers, printers and so forth in my own assignments. Where I have to supervise a piece of work and co-ordinate the final parts, I mark up their work. If it is very straightforward, I don't. With large amounts, I also get my suppliers to invoice clients direct.

> **4** **TIP** If you are using others to help you and their costs are going to be large (printing and market research come quickly to mind), get your suppliers to invoice your client direct. While you won't be able to put a mark-up into the system, it will do wonders for your cash-flow.

I believe that your suppliers (a key part of your network, remember) need to be paid fast. If you pay them and then wait 90 to 120 days for your money (about big company average for payments these days), you are going to be out of pocket and out of funds.

## THE MARK-UP GAME

Over the years I have completed a large number of third-party assignments. These are usually fed to you from big consulting firms who either haven't the time or possibly that specialist expertise to do it themselves. It is always a useful insight into the world that we don't often tread, where fees reach heights most independents can only dream of. Most of my experiences have been bizarre.

I was asked – at 24 hours' notice – to write a speech for a senior executive. So paranoid was the agency about their client, that not only was I not allowed to meet them or get a briefing on the phone, I wasn't even told which company it was for.

Some months later I played golf with a friend and his brother. We got talking after the game and the brother was recounting some humorous stories about his work and told one about this paranoid agency and this speech they had written for him. I quickly realised it was MY speech. So (here we go with the asking again) I asked him if he could recall how much he paid. He told me. It was three times what I had charged. Guess who got the next assignment?!

# Retainer business

In my part of consulting, retainers are but a distant memory. For those who have never come across them, it works like this. A company engages your services (usually for a fixed number of hours or days per month, plus any expense incurred) on a long-term (one- to two-year) agreement. For this you are paid a regular income, usually on the first of the month.

The trouble with retainers is that they are normally rather restrictive. First, they will usually stipulate who else you can and cannot work for. Second, they often end in a huge accumulation of unspent time, which you may find having to work off long after the 'retainer' has expired, depending on the deal you so enthusiastically agreed.

My view, if I was offered a regular retainer today, would be to examine it microscopically from all sides, write my own version and get it witnessed by my legal adviser as well as the client. Then again, if you can get an 'open' retainer, which means if the client doesn't use your time in the course of that month (or time agreed) then it is their loss, go for it. If clients want to be silly with their money, we are not in business to discourage them from doing so.

# Expenses

You could write a book just on expenses, possibly an encyclopaedia. But for the purposes of this book, it is important for any independent to understand that getting reimbursed (quickly) for costly outlays is vital. Again, it is that cash-flow issue that you must be ever aware of.

Always ask for an up-front advance on expenses (usually around 10 to 15 per cent of the fee estimate). This means that you are not turning yourself into a bank for your client, but are using a portion of their money to get a project operational.

Some consultants mark up expenses incurred by adding anything from 15 to 25 per cent to the total – I don't. When I make a proposal, I always make it clear that expenses are billed net (and supported by invoices where required) as incurred and that's it. This must be a good policy. Since 1982, no one has ever refused to pay my expense invoices and no one has ever asked for all those receipts. They may have frowned at a few, I imagine, but never refused to pay!

As a personal thing, I also like to pay for my own travel and then bill it to the client. Often, clients prefer to do it for you (usually because they think they can get better deals than you do), and if you are just starting out don't worry: they are paying and you're not. In the early days, anything that will provide sacrifices to the goddess of cash-flow is very acceptable. More on travel is detailed in Chapter 10.

# Recovering development costs

Depending on the business you are getting into, business development costs (some call them market opportunity costs or cost of sales) can be quite considerable. Most consultants need to create programmes and concepts and these take time and often real monetary expense to develop fully. My view is that anything you do for yourself to enhance and grow the business is a real sunk cost. The way to get it back is to sell your idea. However, being asked by a client or prospect to develop some ideas is a different thing. What I always do is keep a strict record of the time (and the real expense) of such an exercise and build this into the final business proposal. Of course, not every opportunity works out like that, but it does give you some way of recouping your costs and your time.

Again, much depends on what sort of business you are in. If you are in personnel training, you will have a need to create programmes and back-up materials (if only to convince a prospective customer of your professionalism). In this case these are true development costs that may never – in reality – be fully recovered. On the other hand, if a client asks you to develop something, charge them (time and expense) for doing it.

Don't forget, as a consultant, clients will use you because they expect you to have the right ideas, the right programmes, the right information that they require. This means that you have to have a development process (like that new business process) going on all the time.

Other costs include travel to the prospective client's location and doing early research on an idea. Planes, trains and motorcars, as well as hotels and other services needed to sustain us cost money. Try and keep track of it all and assess how well you are doing. Ideally, when you finally make proposals, get as much of this up-front expense in there, so that you can begin to reduce those development costs.

Of course, you may well find yourself involved in making a major (hugely time-consuming proposal) to a prospective client, only to have it turned down flat. Console yourself and consider whether you can approach anyone else with this idea, or adapt it for other uses. Although virtually every proposal I make is a one-off event, there are generally elements that can be re-used or re-developed in different ways. If you become good at this, you can quickly reduce your overall development costs and the time involvement too.

## DEALING WITH NO-SHOWS

Clients and prospective clients can be quite rude. Well, maybe not rude, just unaware of what it takes to do our job. A colleague of mine runs personal development programmes and frequently has real difficulties because two or three from a group of 10 not only don't show, but don't bother to call and say so. This is particularly galling when he is running free 'taster' seminars as part of his marketing effort.

To try to counter this, he came up with a great idea. When you register, you have to pledge that in the event of a no-show, you will donate £25 (by giving your credit card details) to a charity. Not only does this shame people into calling to cancel, it has had the effect of reducing no-shows to a minimum.

# Contracts and letters of engagement

Once someone on the client side has said 'yes', it is time to get a piece of paper put together that clearly states the basic work to be done and the price to be paid for it. So many organisations have their own versions that it is pretty pointless suggesting your own. However, do try and get that set up right from the outset as if something does go wrong, this is your safety-net. All too often (and I am as guilty as the rest) you get enthused and excited about a new assignment and go rushing off to get things started (often the reason for that is the ludicrous time-frame YOU have agreed to!). Try and curb that urge. Get an e-mail or fax version, sign it and keep their version. Then get to work.

In these hectic days things happen fast. Take-overs, mergers, executive departures and organisational changes can all bring havoc to independent activity. That contract or letter of engagement will ensure that you get paid if something goes wrong.

I have to add something to that. In recent years it has become harder than ever for independent consultants to legally tie down work. The sheer complication of today's corporation – and its avowed mission of avoiding litigation as far as possible – means that you as the solo operator can get seriously tied up in just signing off on a contract. While you should be working for the client, you are stuck with reading and rereading contracts and the like. This has become a huge problem for the simple reason that it ties up your time in completely unproductive effort.

# When the brief changes

In recent years, I can't recall a single consulting assignment where the original brief stayed the same throughout the duration of the project. This usually stems from the fact that most clients – but please don't tell them this – rarely have much idea about what they want and consequently give a really bad briefing.

Because of this, most independent consultants find themselves deep into a project when the brief changes and new elements get inserted into the programme. At this time, it is important that the agreement you have clearly states that changes are an additional cost that needs to be quoted for on top of the original proposal. Do this quickly. Call your client. Inform them of the changes that their firm requires and send them a revised budget and time-frame. The sooner this is done the better. Then when the new work is agreed, have that added to the contract or agreement. If you are lucky, they won't create yet another contract and will simply add the modifications to the existing pile of paper.

What you don't want are any (further) protracted negotiations as these just detract from getting the real assignment completed. Again, remember – especially if you are a real solo operator – that time is finite and you should be working, not tied up in contract negotiation. Once it has gone, you can't claw this time back.

Although you can waste large amounts of time, I've never found it useful to bill every last cent. If I am working on an assignment for say 15 days and I run over a day, I won't bill that extra time. I will, however, make sure the client knows how generous I am. If I finish that 15-day assignment in 14 days, I won't give him back any money either; so it is very much swings and roundabouts – some you win, some they win. Remember that it is always important to keep time sheets for each assignment (even if the client never wants to see them) so you can assess the actual cost of the project. Very often in my business I am quoting 'blind'. That is to say I am putting together a quote for a client based on a request that I have never had before (and very often something they have never done before either). Hopefully, I am experienced enough to get it about right, but the only way I know that I haven't screwed myself is to keep a daily track of how much time I have spent.

## The gentle art of quoting

Just like selling, some independent consultants are naturally good at getting this right. Others are – and seem to remain – woefully inadequate and never get any better at it. The key to getting the quote right is a complex formula that actually has very little to do with reality and a lot to do with perception – the client's perception. If they feel they are getting value for money, that's all that counts from their side. This is another reason for working with major firms, as they usually know how to buy consulting and they are expecting to pay for it.

Never allow yourself to get talked into anything where payment is dependent on results. It is YOUR time that you are selling and therefore that is what you are quoting for. However, the formula is complex. When you are eager to get a piece of business, you will be sorely tempted to reduce the number of days or squeeze down your hourly charges. This is not good as it sets a bad precedent. Every time I have been worried about getting business in and have reduced a budget, another piece of business (at a much better rate of pay) has come along. What happens (and I tell my clients this too), is that you concentrate on the new piece of well-remunerated work and the other piece comes a poor second. That old phrase that a labourer is worthy of his hire is very true. So when you quote, think about reality. What is it really going to take in terms of time to do the best job you can? Once you've worked that one out, stick to it.

# Evolving the client relationship

The smart consultant knows that once he is inside the corporate version of Troy, his secondary task must be to stay there. This isn't that hard. Presenteeism works better for consultants than anyone else. The fact that you are in front of the XYZ's executives on a regular basis means that your chances of other assignments increase dramatically. Just because you are there, you will be given work, because it is a lot easier to give it to you than start over the process of searching for someone who is really qualified to do it. So, the trick is to build confidence and reputation and volunteer a lot for assignments.

In my experience, really busy managers are just relieved to get assignments off their desks and into some kind of action mode. If this may sound a little cynical, it really isn't. Once a client gets to know you and your capabilities, they will feel comfortable and like having you around. Encourage this and develop strong relationships. I know consultants who regularly take their clients to football, cricket and tennis events or have London theatre evenings. Very often hard-pressed executives are grateful for these 'excursions', which underscore how much you value the relationship.

> **5** **TIP** In the twenty-first century, the business environment can change very quickly. So don't put too many beans in that tin please. Keep as wide a range of clients and prospects as you can – you'll need them one day. Think not? Oh, YES you will.

# Getting paid

In my experience, most companies are fairly good at paying what they owe. There are exceptions, but you rapidly learn how to avoid doing business with these people. However, the most important thing about getting paid is up to you. It is simply getting your invoice in on time. Do not delay. As soon as you can get it in for approval – do it. The main reason for this is that the modern corporation takes anything from 60–150 days to pay, so you want to give yourself the very best chance you can, otherwise cash flow (yes, there we are again) can be seriously compromised.

> 6 **TIP** Invoice as rapidly as you can, it can make at least 30 days' difference to when you get paid.

I have to say that in a career of over two decades, I have only had two bad debts that I had to write off totally. In both cases the people went out of business, leaving huge debts and there was nothing to be recovered. Luckily each of these was for small amounts.

At other times, circumstances just catch up with you. A case in point was early in my solo career when I encountered what I would describe as the independent consultant's black hole. My client – a senior manager in a major multinational – was made redundant very suddenly. I had an agreement with him – including a working contract – but it had not yet been approved by his boss (the one who terminated him). I had done a great deal of work and had already billed for two-thirds of the assignment. I had never met my client's boss. The only thing to do was go and see him. I got a meeting arranged and flew to Paris and explained the situation in some detail. Perhaps I was lucky, I don't know, but he arranged for all that was owed to be paid that day. Personally, I believe that the act of going to see him made the difference. This is really worth remembering. Although you may find the confrontation difficult, if you can go and see the person involved (the one that can pay you), it is worth the effort for one single reason – it legitimises your case. You get to meet, you get to talk and explain. That's important – especially when you are a solo operator.

Similarly, I read with horror a newspaper account of a corporate meltdown at one of my clients where I had a string of unpaid invoices. In the midst of a mass redundancy programme, I again reached the managing director of one of the divisions and he personally took me to the accounts department and got my invoices paid in full. Personal relationships (and your client's PA) count big-time in these circumstances.

## CREATING EMBARRASSMENT

Some years ago a relatively small firm owed me money. I knew they were in financial trouble and was concerned that they would eventually go out of business leaving us with nothing after we had completed all the work. Phone calls, reminders and threats of legal action failed. So I had an idea. We had a cross-town courier service we used and one of their people was the meanest person I had ever laid eyes on (he looked like a former boxer who had fallen on hard times). In reality he was a really nice person, but most people just looked at him and ran. What I did was to offer him 10 per cent of this outstanding invoice if he could collect. On his day off he turned up in the accounts department of the firm and asked for the money. They told him to wait. He did. Telling everyone else that came in that he was trying to collect the money and he wasn't going home without it. After two hours he emerged, a cheque for full payment in hand. We deposited it in the bank within 10 minutes to make sure it didn't bounce!

## A SUITCASE FULL OF TROUBLE

Sometimes independents really have to think out of the box to get the money they have worked for. I had completed a major project for a London-based publisher. Although I had received my initial payment, two-thirds of the fees and the majority of the final expenses were still to be paid and they had just been taken over by a rival after an acrimonious series of negotiations. My concern was getting paid in full. What I did was to arrive in London with a suitcase that contained all the manuscripts they required. I then sat in a café until their office boy appeared with a cheque. I then took him and my suitcase to a bank where I had arranged to deposit the money. Once it was deposited I handed the office boy the suitcase. Rather extreme, but as it turned out, probably necessary. Six months later the new owners went out of business. This further proves my point that working for large companies (or the public sector) is the best idea for a long-term career as an independent consultant.

What all this illustrates is that you need to really know your client and the risks that may be involved in working with them. Relationships and working styles vary hugely from place to place. A major multinational is very different from a consulting firm or the public sector. Chances are that you will experience all of these and more in your independent career. Understanding the differences is part of your guide to survival and ultimate success. While you may never work for or with all of them, there are very rewarding experiences to be had and an assignment in one can lead to a huge learning experience which can often transfer to another sector. Yes, you can build up some great, trusting relationships, but business is a highly volatile world – things happen when you least expect them.

# Working with different client groups

You are going to find yourself – most probably – in a wide variety of work environments. I hope so. One of the most satisfying parts of an independent consultant's life (unless you really are a shy retiring flower) is being able to experience different work places, patterns and probably politics too. Below, I have outlined some thoughts on different employer groups, which may give you some ideas as you begin to widen your work horizons.

## *The big corporations*

Most of my consulting work has been for major multinationals. Depending on your expertise, this can be hugely rewarding both in job satisfaction and remuneration. Obviously it demands a great deal of flexibility and usually travel away from home base for periods of time. For me this is more than compensated by the variety and scale of the work and the opportunities for ongoing learning and development that these sorts of assignment generate.

While it can be difficult to break in, the best way is often on the back of a bigger consulting firm that needs extra arms and legs on major assignments. When the bigger consulting firms get busy, they are often only too pleased to have third parties they can call on for help. It really is worthwhile going to see these people. To cite one example, I have a colleague who has become a global traveller through lending his skills to due diligence efforts for acquisitive corporations. In these cases he is hired and paid by the firm's consultants. Getting in at the ground level for these type of assignments is not that easy, but if this is your sort of thing, the effort is well worth it.

Big corporations today don't have the army of internal support functions that they used to. Increasingly, areas like training and development, coaching, mentoring, market research, communications and so on are outsourced. This kind of 'give it out to others' activity doesn't take place solely at the headquarters but in divisions scattered around the globe. Getting the initial foot in the door might not be easy, but smart corporations are constantly on the look-out for specialists who can help them.

> 7 **TIP** Don't be discouraged or too concerned just because it is a big multinational business. Often these places are a lot less sophisticated than you might think.

## The big consultants

The major consultants often use third-party help when the going gets busy. Indeed, I know several independents that work virtually exclusively for one or two big firms, using their unique talents to help meet client needs. Very often some type of specialist knowledge that you can sell, or your experience of a particular industry or region, can get you hired.

## SMEs

Depending on your skills and career plans, any independent consultant can make a good living out of working for small and medium-sized enterprises. If you want to work within a particular geography, for example, it makes a great deal of sense to become established in a specific community. Certainly, getting business by word of mouth is more likely when working within a restricted geographic area. Joining local chambers of commerce and other trade-related groups also gets your face in front of the local business community. The only warning I would give is to make sure that you thoroughly check out the financial viability of prospective clients. Of course, major multinationals go bust as well, but not with the same fatal consistency as smaller firms. But then again, they do get merged or acquired a lot these days.

## Public sector

Although I have little experience of the public sector, I do know consultants who have gleaned almost all their business from this area. I know two management consultants who have built up a lucrative practice advising local government on operational management issues as well as a consultant in healthcare who has established herself firmly within the National Health Service. Again, it is all a question of getting your foot in the door. Often assignments are given out to tender – especially in local government – and it is worthwhile checking out opportunities. A simple visit to your local council offices (or their website) may unearth more than you expected. Additionally, local libraries and local newspapers usually advertise upcoming opportunities.

### NGOs

Non-governmental organisations are on the increase both nationally and internationally and virtually all use consultants. While I know of many consultants who do this work because they are also in tune with the NGO's aims, they still can provide a solid income and a very rewarding career path. In many cases – in both national and international operations – the management of NGOs is excellent and they like to work within very specific guidelines and with clear-cut and precise contracts. If this type of career appeals to you, I suggest surfing the web as the best way of getting to know what NGOs require in the way of external consultant support.

### *Transnational institutions*

By this I mean everything from the European Union and the United Nations to the World Health Organisation and the World Bank. These types of institutions constantly spawn new initiatives and need outside help in carrying them out. Again, get access (use the web) to their official publications, which explain a great deal about their current work and plans. I know several specialist independent consultants who seem to work exclusively for this type of institution. From my own experience, it seems to be a question of working hard to get inside but once you are there, you are pretty secure for quite some time.

# Developing long-term client relationships

While we are going to look in-depth at developing your business in Chapter 8, it is worth saying a few words here about how to develop a long-term relationship with a client. First, what you have to get clear in your mind is whether this is a relationship based on an individual who feeds you work, or with the organisation that he or she works for. Ideally you can have both. Getting business these days can be hard work, so you want to get the most out of all your efforts. Therefore, I think that the most important aspect of evolving a business relationship is to try and spread yourself through a business and not be reliant on one person to give you work.

Part of that reason is straightforward. If your corporate champion gets transferred, promoted or leaves, what happens then? If you are already known to others, then you have a much better chance of surviving. That, of course, does not always happen. Too often your client leaves and is replaced with a new manager who brings not only his own ideas but his own external consultants with him. That is the nightmare scenario for all of us independents and one we can do little about. At that point our only recourse is to follow our old client and hope that he or she has work for us in their new job.

One of the biggest barriers to developing and enlarging a client relationship is often our own failure to get across what we really do. When I analyse it (usually when it is too late!), I realise that I was hired for a specific task, using me for something they could not do easily for themselves. Where I failed often was not to let my clients know of all the other skills I have available. For example, if I get hired to work on some employee communications strategy, they are not going to ask me to write the chairman's speech to the shareholders unless they know that's what I also do. It is this failure to advertise ourselves (when we have already sold ourselves) that probably loses independent consultants more business than anything else.

# Conflict of interest

I have had countless conversations with fellow consultants about what constitutes a conflict of interest. My 'rule' is that I will only ever work exclusively for an organisation in an industry if it has me on a full retainer or a long-term contract. There is a tacit 'gentlemen's agreement' whereby in the course of undertaking work on behalf of an organisation, that you won't divulge to third parties any interesting snippets of information you may hear or read about, however tempting it might be. Other views also prevail. Head-hunters would be instantly swept out of business if they followed the 'you can only work for one client in each industry' rule, that some firms try to impose. Where possible, I feel very comfortable (and usually ask) to sign a non-disclosure or confidentiality agreement with my clients. But today, it would be practically impossible to work for just one company in an industry and we have to rely on our professional reputations and be known as someone 'who keeps his counsel' to get us through.

> **8** **TIP** Your reputation is like your virginity – you only lose it once.

## THE VANISHING DEPARTMENT

Life for the independent consultant is not always easy. At times it takes on a farcical tone. Some years ago, I had – after long, protracted discussions – sold a large research project to a major consulting firm. One Thursday evening, I left their offices with a plan to come back on the Monday morning to finalise contracts and begin the work. When I got to reception on the Monday, I asked for my contact. The receptionist looked a little surprised and then flustered. She made a few phone calls and finally a man appeared. By this time the reception area was filling up with visitors. My 'host' escorted me to a side office where he explained that my contact was no longer with the firm – he had been made redundant on the Friday after my Thursday meeting! When I asked after the others on the 'new' team I was working with, they had gone too. Indeed, a few quick calls on my mobile confirmed that the entire marketing department had 'vanished' overnight. They had been so traumatised by the whole experience that no one had thought to call me.

And no, I never did get any more business from that firm. This story goes to show that it is NEVER in the bag until the day you have been paid.

# Paying suppliers

I am scrupulous about paying people who work for me or provide goods and services. Reason? They are usually small too and so need to be paid. Alternatively, they are so big, like your phone company, that they will give you all kinds of hassle if you don't pay quickly. Also, pay your small supplier fast and you will be their friend forever, which is very useful when you need them in a hurry. Think about it. Who would you drop everything for – the client who pays you in 30 days or the one that pays in 120?

In any case, getting a reputation as a poor or late payer isn't good for your image and just isn't worth it. This is another reason to make sure that you maintain a healthy cash-flow, so that you can be sure of paying all your suppliers on time.

# Agents and alliances

There will come a time when someone does you a big favour that results in a very nice piece of business for you. The question then is how to thank them. Personally, I find it best to enter into some sort of formal or informal arrangement. On that sort of basis, a payment of between 10 and 20 per cent of the fees you receive is the most usual. This usually lasts for a period of 12 months.

In other cases, fees vary from 10 per cent in year one, to 7.5 per cent in year two and 5 per cent in year three. This of course makes it complicated to administer and I much prefer to pay a one-time flat fee per assignment. All my relationships like this are based on trust (which incidentally has to work both ways).

I have a series of these alliances and also our FutureWork Forum group operates on the same basis. In that case, one of our members is the leader for that assignment and carries out all the invoicing and administration. Any other member of the Forum who gets involved gets paid for their time accordingly.

> **TIP** The same obviously applies if you, as the consultant, are able to sell a project for another consultant. In this case, there are various ways to be remunerated, but I like to keep it simple and usually expect 10 per cent over the first year of any assignment (that is always for fees only).

To give you some idea of what an agreement looks like, Appendix A sets out a sample version that I have used effectively for some years.

Now we have reached a watershed point. You are established, you have clients, a viable business with a little money tucked away. So what now? How do you develop the business? Move on to Chapter 8 and you'll see.

# Key learning points

> Learn the clients' rules and play by them.
> Set fees and stick to them, except under the direst of circumstances.

> Independents can easily have variable fees to suit the type of work they are asked to do.

> Give prospective clients one free meeting, then decide how you play it. Try and charge for your time from meeting two.

> Never give away all your ideas in a proposal, keep something back to give you security.

> Remember, if it looks too good to be true – IT IS!

> Get a contract – especially for new business.

> When making proposals: make it original; make it short; make it formal; wait 24 hours to check it out AND CHECK THE SPELLING.

> Make the Personal Assistant your pal, they are the link to the client.

> Never, ever agree to be paid by results. Your time is precious, get rewarded for using it.

> Unless you are on a retainer, a conflict of interest should not arise. If it does, weigh your options: just how much do you want to be locked in?

> Always pay small suppliers as quickly as you can. A reputation as a good payer is the best one to have.

> Agents and other 'business-getters' will expect a minimum of 10 per cent of any business they bring you. Remember, this is a percentage of fees only.

# Chapter **8**

# Developing the business

'Appearances count. Get a sun lamp ... maintain an elegant address even if you have to live in the attic. Never nickle and dime when you're short of cash.'

**Aristotle Onassis**

'I keep six honest serving men
(They taught me all I knew)
Their names are What and Why and When
And How and Where and Who.'

**Rudyard Kipling**

So, you've made it! You have created a stable, sustainable business. You have clients who appreciate your skills and counsel. You have a network that you resolutely maintain. You have some cash in the bank and things are not looking too bad at all. So what happens next?

The answer to that depends entirely on who you are and what you want to achieve in the future. For example, if you are content to stay as a solo operator and be a healthy yet small fish in a small pond, or even a small, very special type of fish in the big pond, that's fine. Well, it is fine until the day you change your mind at least.

On the other hand, if you want to do new things and take the business in new directions and search for new consulting worlds to conquer, you are going to have to think long and hard about how to achieve that. However, in my experience, you rarely have that clean-cut choice of whether to stick with what you know or change for something different or new.

Quite simply, your business changes. Every day something about your business is not quite the same as the day before. Just like a giant corporation, your little independent consulting firm is under pressure. And pressure bends things into new shapes. If we don't evolve, we will find ourselves with a business that doesn't meet the needs of our clientele; certainly not the way it used to. And that is easy to understand. All we need to consider is the impact of just one thing – technology – on our business to realise that over the years that pressure has pushed and pulled us in all sorts of new directions.

Furthermore, our clients will demand new ideas, new solutions, new methods of working. If we are to remain successful, we have to be able to meet and hopefully exceed those demands and expectations.

All of us – on a day-to-day, week-to-week basis – have to be aware of the evolving needs of the marketplace in which we operate, and how we respond to the next set of challenges placed before us. We need to make choices about which direction to take next, what investments we need to make, and what new skills we need to acquire. You can be sure of one thing: some time in the next 24 months, demand for part of what you offer the business community will slow down (or disappear forever). When that happens, what are you going to replace it with?

It could be a simple change in the law that offers tax credits for learning on a huge scale that prompts the rise of a host of new competitors; or an emerging technology that threatens to automate one of your processes and remove your competitive edge. Whatever it is, you need to be ready to change to meet that sort of challenge. And in talking to independent consultants with all sorts of skills sets and talents, it quickly becomes clear that everyone is vulnerable and that our long-term success depends on surviving in a world of constant, ever more rapid, change.

Sure, we all know people who have been doing the same thing for the past 10 years. But I bet none of us knows anyone who has been doing the same thing – and dispensing the same advice – for 20 years. And, in today's world, for how long can decade-old advice be relevant anyway?

The key to survival as an independent consultant today is all about being ready to change your game when the time comes. My own career is a case in point. I began by doing as a freelance what I had done inside corporations – communications work. My early days were based around speechwriting and article preparation. As a lot of this activity within big business declined in the late 1980s, I moved up a few gears and began research work on business issues. That lasted for another 10 years or so. I then began to create my business book-writing career and through that, my platform career as a so-called expert on the issues I had been researching. All of that happened gradually (there was no sudden shift in emphasis), with a steady phase-out of certain activities. If I look around today at other successful independents who have survived the ups and downs of the economic roller-coaster, they have all been able to change their game as it became necessary. None of them is doing what they did 20 years ago.

Any business, YOUR business, needs to move forward to maintain its vitality and its ability to serve clients in the best way possible. You can do this in several ways:

> Stay as a solo operator, but remain constantly aware of the market's shifting sands and be prepared to quickly do something about it.
> Form an alliance, joint venture or partnership with others.
> Hire in people (pitfalls in doing that).
> Contract out (pitfalls in doing that).
> Consciously shrink the business.

Let's look at these in more detail (there are guides to the legal issues in Chapter 11).

# The solo operator

I know many solo operator consultancies, where the person is only too pleased to remain that way. They may ask for outside help on an ad hoc basis, but essentially they remain true independents. There is nothing at all wrong with this. Many of those I know make a good living doing work that they really like (often they are highly specialised, even within a narrow niche of expertise). The only advice that I would give them is to make sure they stay up to date with their own special area of expertise. Interestingly, this is something most of them do by habit, as in many cases they make most of their income from working for other consultants who don't want – or can't afford – to develop that type of expertise in-house. Sudden change is unlikely to concern them as they seem to evolve along with the businesses they consult to. All the same, they are vulnerable to a major change in the way of doing business or if what they do loses its popularity.

# Alliances, joint ventures and partnerships

Too many independents have made the fatal mistake of hooking up with others and finding that they have lost the 'soul' of their own business in the process. My advice is to begin if possible with a loose alliance (so no legal commitments and no share swaps). If that works, then consider just how compatible you will be in the long term. Let the initial euphoria of discovering a fellow-traveller evaporate and then assess, very honestly, how sound you think this venture will look in five years' time.

I maintain several **alliances** with other consultants whom I respect and feel comfortable working with. But, after my own bitter experience of a partnership, I will keep it just that – an oral agreement, that we both understand. There is no reason that these sort of loose alliances cannot last for many years without requiring any kind of formalisation. For the independent consultant who values their independence, it is probably all that is required. The huge upside is that you can make your own decisions on who you work with, who you work for and just what direction you want the business to go. Remember, as soon as you link up with someone else, your ability to make decisions entirely on your own is compromised. Do you really want that to happen?

**Joint ventures** and **partnerships** demand a lot more in terms of commitment, as well as throwing up lots of legal issues. You need a great deal of good advice before you plunge into one of these. Taking time to really understand the other parties' motives for the deal pays off.

Recently, I witnessed a two-man independent firm sensibly, in my view, backing off from an alliance with a US consulting group. All was well in the early wooing stages. Then it became increasingly clear that their cosy world (where they made their own decisions and set their own work times) would be deeply affected by any formal relationship. The first inkling of trouble was when they discovered that they were spending a huge amount of time in transatlantic conference calls setting sales and business development targets. As one of them told me, 'In all these hours talking about doing business, we could have been doing it, instead of just talking about it.'

This move to be part of a more formal structure can easily be a setback to those of us who are true independents at heart. Certainly, there is an increase in 'staff' meetings, reports, memos, budgeting and the like. All that time takes away from the process of meeting client needs.

The other huge downside – for me at least – is that loss of being able to do what I want when I want. You will recall that in the early chapters of the book I mentioned how important it was to establish what kind of independent you want to be. I gave examples of consultants who work one day a week or take two weeks in every three off. Once you have a partner or partners, it isn't as easy to set your own work times. There is much more need for presenteeism – just being around the workplace – than when you are on your own. Think long and hard before you plunge in.

# Hiring staff

The easy answer to this is to just SAY 'no!'. But that is hardly a practical piece of advice. Unless you know that you have long-term work assignments that are signed, sealed and set in stone, think carefully about a move of this kind. As every independent knows, hiring staff falls under the same category as buying a boat: there are two great moments, the day you buy it and the day you sell it. With staff it is easy to hire, not always so easy to fire. Legal aspects of employment (not the least social security costs) make the exercise an increasingly tough proposition for the small firm.

Consider carefully what this new member of your business is going to do. Could a contract worker do it as well? Will they be fully occupied? Will they be capable of developing themselves and your business?

On good days it gives you a nice feeling to see your team toiling away. On others it produces dark clouds of concern. If you cannot guarantee that you can fully occupy them five days a week, think of another solution. Also, when you hire them, ask yourself a question: 'Will they be able to help develop the business?' For the small consulting firm, this is a vital attribute. Indeed, unless you are just adding some type of personal assistant, any other hire needs to bring in business and pay for themselves (or at least part of their upkeep). In doing that, they can often play to their strengths and open up new lines of opportunity, which you couldn't do on your own.

So think carefully before you go down this route. Having built up a business and employed a fair number of people, there is nothing so depressing as realising each month that you have to generate enough business to pay them all. That's not what you got into business for is it? Hire people and you will quickly discover that you have just placed yourself – as chief business-getter – on an unstoppable treadmill. There is nothing worse than seeing your staff going home on a Friday afternoon, or taking a week off at Christmas, while you have to knuckle down and try and keep the business coming in.

> **1** **TIP** When you hire, try to take on someone who, while being in tune with how you do business, has some attributes or skills you don't have. This really can help 'round out' a small firm.

## Contracting out

If you cannot justify the outright hiring of employees, then it is far better to develop some long-term links with those that can help you. The upside to this is quite clear. The most important advantage is that it gives you flexibility. You can hire people on short-term agreements and then wait until another assignment comes in before using them again. If you analyse this type of contract activity over a year or more, you should see that it is a lot more cost-effective than having people permanently on the payroll, whom you have to remunerate whether they are doing client work or not.

Certainly in this increasingly outsourced age, using contract workers is a growing trend. As I pointed out earlier, many specialist consultants make their living on contracts from other businesses.

So flexibility and cost are the two main advantages, and often these contractual deals can develop into long-term working relationships. However, as with everything else, there are some downsides too. The two main ones are loyalty and availability.

While you cannot expect anything like 100 per cent loyalty from anyone you use as a contractor, you need to be careful (especially in the early days of a relationship) just how much information you wish to share. Back to that 'don't tell people your secrets' issue. Time and again, I have heard the sad news that yet another independent colleague has been 'done over' by one of his contracted helpers. This is usually through letting them get too close to the client and taking over the work (often at promised – but rarely ever realised – savings). It is a hard, cruel world out there, and some people will do almost anything to secure business.

> **2** **TIP** Keep your 'casual' contractors at arm's length from your clients until your relationship is well established and fully understood.

The other issue is availability. Possibly the only real advantage of having people on your payroll is that they are there to work for you alone (it is, of course, your job to keep them gainfully employed) and so the issue of availability doesn't really arise. However, working with outsourced workers means that you cannot always guarantee that they will have the time available when you need it.

The solution is to find several people that you really like to work with and then give them enough business to 'buy' their loyalty and their availability. You will quickly know what that takes for different people. But don't forget that if you don't use someone for months on end, you will probably have to do that trust-building exercise all over again.

Personally, I would much rather work with a squad of carefully chosen contract workers (so I can get the best niche consultant or specialist for whatever I need) rather than hire people and try to make them do everything. This certainly isn't everyone's view and I am sure it depends on your style of working and your long-term objectives for the business.

# Shrinking the business

Ask a range of successful consultants to name the time they were happiest (not richest or most successful, but happiest) and most will tell you it was when they started out. Despite all the hard work and wondering if they would make it, life, in retrospect at least, seemed simpler and more focused. Not surprising then that many consultants who have built up highly successful practices often consider the idea of going back to the solo life again. There are a large number of reasons for this, but often it is that quest for a better quality of life or, as I mentioned earlier in the book, a chance to pursue other interests.

I took the decision to shrink my own business some years ago. Starting out on my own and building up to a group of around 15 people was fun. But those early years trying to make it on my own were perhaps the best. Now I work alone again, carrying out assignments that interest me and give me opportunities to meet and be involved with interesting organisations and individuals. In that, I consider myself lucky. I have been able to go, in a career of 30 plus years, from corporate life, to independent consultant, to business owner and back to a solo operator. Hopefully, I am wiser now. Also my network has grown and, as I have been stressing throughout this book, has been assiduously maintained and added to year on year.

There is never a right time to become – or return to the life of – a solo consultant. It is all a question of what is right for you. What it takes is to stay as honest with yourself as you can. Recently I met a series of newly independent consultants – all with successful careers behind them – who decided to reinvent themselves again as solo operators, in order to attain a less stressful life. For many, this seems to involve (as in my case) a move from a city to the country. In the last few years, the profile of my own neighbours where I live has changed from employees commuting to work to a series of independents happily – and I hope successfully – pursuing their new solo careers.

## Checking out the marketplace

Whichever way you decide to go to develop the business, you must keep up to date. Membership – and possibly an active interest – in professional associations can help, if only for the opportunity to 'steal' ideas from your colleagues! The market does move; new ideas, trends and opportunities come and shake up our established view of our chosen professional area. So knowing what is going on – and what others are doing about it – is vital.

Equally, being aware of world events and putting those into a context that applies to your business can help you to spot emerging trends before they impact on you too much. I also believe that clients appreciate a consultant who seems to know what is going on in the big wide world and can relate that easily to their business. It just makes them feel that little bit more comfortable employing you.

What that means is investing in information delivery. While the world wide web can be a source of a lot of material, I still think that the hard-copy written word makes you read (well it does for me). I also find it useful to tear out pieces that interest me and take with me when I travel. I do a lot of my catch-up reading time on trains and planes.

What you choose to read depends on your specific business activity. But if you are involved in any way with consulting outside your own country or in an international context, then you may find it useful to look at my own reading list.

> Each morning and evening (and more frequently if I am working from my home work space) I use the BBC news website – just to be aware of what is happening: http://news.bbc.co.uk.

- Every morning (as I have for the past 30 years) I read the *International Herald Tribune*, because it is the quickest way to get world coverage of issues.
- Similarly I read (or rather scan) the *Financial Times*.
- Every week I get *Business Week*, and more recently I have been taking the UK publication *The Week*.
- Other subscriptions that add to my professional view of the world include *Fortune, Harvard Business Review* and the *New York Review of Books*.

All these keep me up to date in the more general areas of world affairs but also report in-depth on areas that I am most active in and need to know about. In addition, I read a lot of junk stuff too (and also watch MTV and other specialist TV channels) to stay in touch with emerging trends and understand better the changing world of work. I am a sort of magazine junky and will read anything and everything. I find that all of it helps me in my day-to-day work because it provides ideas, contacts, lines on new trends that keep you ahead of your clients – which is where you want to be.

There is no substitute to being well informed and no excuse for not being aware of areas and issues that may affect your clients. It can certainly be the 'decider' between you or someone else winning an assignment. The other issue is that if you want to make presentations or write articles to impress your peers and prospects, you'll be much more persuasive if you can put your expertise into a world context. If you don't know what's going on, you can't do that.

# Keeping up to speed

Just as the media play an important role in keeping you up to speed with world and industry affairs that affect your clients, so personal development helps you to be a much more useful consultant. By that I mean that your role is not just to give advice and counsel, you need to go back to school occasionally and take some instruction too. Seminars, workshops, conferences and debates are all important for keeping you aware of what your profession is up to and also how you may need to change the way you work or the service you offer.

Likewise, personal development programmes help to focus on areas of self-improvement. Rather like getting a health check, it is a good idea to sign yourself up for some type of personal development programme (if only because, for a few days, it will get you out of the professional rut that we all fall into sooner or later).

Indeed, many independent consultants say that they don't go to professional conferences or even development seminars for the content but just as an opportunity to reflect on where they are going and what they really want to do. Down-time, for even the most eager solo operator, is a good thing.

## Marketing others

If you have found yourself hiring staff, you are going to have to make some quick choices about whether or not you want to sell their services. While this depends to a great extent on what their role is, if they have any kind of contact with the client, you need to make sure that they are an asset to the business rather than a turn-off. You know what is expected by the client; your new hire (or even your contracted helper) doesn't. This can make for difficult relationships as you try to ensure that this new person not only fits in with your way of working, but also is respected and appreciated by your clients. Over the years, I have had all sorts of problems with this (everything from poor – to completely inappropriate – dress sense, to basic attitude), and it is never easy to resolve, without some hurt feelings.

Try to develop your new hire's contact with clients on a slow, but steady learning curve, ironing out any bumps along the way. And don't forget the very basic rule: this is YOUR business and YOUR clients. Manage them both the way you see fit. Don't compromise. If a new hire – or new contractor – can't work the way you would like, remove them. In the longer term you'll have to anyway. It will just cause a lot more trouble to delay the decision.

> **3** **TIP** Never forget that with a small consultancy the client is buying YOU. If you add personnel he is still buying YOU. How you manage your people is your problem. Do it badly and it will reflect on you.

## Keeping your culture

It may sound a little grandiose to talk about culture in a one- or two-man outfit – but not so. You created your own culture from the moment you made that decision to strike out on your own. Therefore, it is really important that as soon as you seek to add other people to your firm, that they truly understand what your consulting services stand for. If they don't 'get it', you won't be able to properly retain that cultural 'feel' that may have taken you years to create and that your clients appreciate so much. So, keep the culture intact. Make it clear from Day One (write it down if necessary) that these are your cultural mores and the way you do business. Make sure your new associates or employees sign up to this.

# Have you lost focus?

While many independents have built up strikingly successful 'boutique' consulting firms from very modest beginnings and are able to thrive and prosper, others come to realise that this often takes them away from their primary reasons for starting up in the first place. I know of many independents who created a business, only to find that they had removed themselves from the day to day, hands-on part of the operation.

'It just stopped being fun,' one told me. 'After 10 years of growing the business, I realised all I was doing was working like hell to bring in business to feed the people I had hired.' Another, who created an award-winning design consulting firm told me, 'One day I realised that in the past six months all I had done with a pen in my hand was to sign expenses for my employees!'

In both these cases, the consultants went back to their roots and their real reason for starting up, being involved in the day-to-day action and solving challenging problems. Keeping a sense of focus and knowing why you are in this business is important and you should never lose sight of that. As another consultant who had recently returned to single operator status explained, 'I just wasn't happy. I had everything I thought I should have. Then I realised the buzz had gone. The reason when I sat down and thought about it was that I wasn't made for managing others. I was made for getting things done – my way.'

Many independent consultants are not great team members – that's why they strike out on their own. So it becomes difficult for them to manage others and they certainly don't enjoy it.

> **TIP** Make it an annual or six-monthly event. Take a day off and sit and think about where you are today, where you've come from and where you REALLY want to go. What's going to make you happy? Do you need to make changes? If so, how long will you give yourself to achieve them?

Recently on a plane to Inverness in Scotland, my fellow passenger turned out to be an independent consulting veterinary surgeon. He had built up a highly successful inner-city practice until one day he realised this was not what he wanted. He knew enough people (that network again!) to get a flow of work mainly from government departments. He now lives and works from his house bordering a Scottish lochside, but travels the world researching and lecturing for his Westminster clients.

# Changing pricing structures

Several times a year I meet recently independent consultants who tell me that business is good – better than they ever dared hope – but they are working all hours of the day and night to meet the demands of their clients. To their question, 'What should I do, Mike?' I have a quick albeit trite response: 'Put up your fees'.

There's a theory held by some of us, and proved by many of us (see box below) that fees are what you want to make them. Slavishly monitoring the market and then following the average price is no more scientific to my mind than sticking a pin in a column of figures. Basically, people who want you will pay you what they think you are worth. True, in economic down-turns there will be pressure on prices, but that should not mean that you are reluctant to return to a good stiff (yet honest) hourly or daily rate as soon as you can. Even if you have been screwed down or held back by cur-rent clients, you should always begin anew with those you are signing on for the first time.

This is one of the great 'secrets' of the independent consultant. You aren't bound by stringent fee structures like many larger firms. If you work for a medium or large consulting firm, you can't easily return to your boss and say, 'well I couldn't get our day rate, but they did agree to one that is 25 per cent less.' Your boss – whose annual bonus is normally cal-culated on fee turnover – would not be best pleased, to say the least.

As individual consultants – or even small boutique firms – we can (and usually do) operate on a sliding scale of prices. This allows you to take on interesting work that may not pay the best rates, but can lead to other opportunities. It also allows you to work in different categories of business.

For example (and I hope I don't live to regret saying this), if I am work-ing for a major multinational corporation I will charge a higher fee (or rather my usual fee) for any work I do. However, there are other small firms, where I am interested in the work but know I will never receive my 'usual', full-fee rate. So I compromise and usually everyone's happy.

**THE 50 PER CENT SOLUTION**

Note that this only works in good economic times. If you are really busy and working all hours, put up your prices by 50 per cent on the next quote you give your client. There is a good chance they won't even notice if they too are very busy.

My colleagues and I have tried this over the years and it always works in terms of total bottom line, because even if you lose 25 per cent of your business, you work less but still make the same overall fee income. *Warning*: As I said, don't try this in a recession, or when your client is mad at you!

5 **TIP** Never publish your fees. Keep them flexible, it opens up opportunities. Big firms expect to pay top dollar (in my experience they don't do 'cheap'. And, YES, you can quote too low, believe me). On the other hand, small firms expect a decent rate, but often this leads to extended business.

# Become a guru?

Another way to develop the business – particularly for the solo operator – is to become a recognised expert in your chosen field. Write a book or a manual, conduct a new line of research and publish it. All of these open up opportunities for the independent to become a recognised expert in their chosen industry. Often authors find themselves in demand for conferences and seminars (at excellent fee levels) and this can provide a useful – often long-lasting – income stream.

As with many things in the independent's life, the big issue is breaking through the barrier and getting published. Once there, it seems easier to keep on doing it. In most cases it takes the development of a fairly unique idea or – for some – jumping on a bandwagon and riding the trend ahead of the pack. As someone once commented, if you see a parade coming down the street, step out and march in front of it!

6 **TIP** If you want to become an industry guru, make sure you get some help in presentation skills.

Of course, becoming a recognised expert isn't for everyone. It certainly helps if you are a good, confident presenter. It also helps if you can put easily understood, attractive presentations together. You'd be amazed how many intelligent consultants turn up at conferences with ill-considered presentation materials. Then there is also 'death by PowerPoint', the overkill of just too many pieces of information.

Once established, industry gurus seem to have a fairly long shelf-life and it can definitely boost your consulting credentials no end. But, remember, make sure you find a relatively unique area to operate in. The market is already crowded, you need a unique selling point.

## Working with the competition

These days, I am not too sure what a competitor really is, so I am very open to working with just about anyone, as long as they have a decent reputation and it is going to be an interesting project. In fact, this can be a good way of boosting your business. All of us get busy at certain times and we certainly don't want to turn work away (as I said earlier, it never comes back). Therefore, if you can get a working agreement with one or more of your competitors to help them out when they have a rush on (and the same in reverse), there is nothing wrong in doing this. Where issues of confidentiality come into the equation or it is a particularly sensitive assignment, always try to clear it with the client. But if it is basic boiler-plate work – as long as you have control over the final output – it can be a useful and practical solution, where everyone wins.

## Nightmare strategies

Every independent consultant – even the very best – have had their equivalent of a Black Monday. That dreaded day when the bottom falls out of the market and all your clients go into an emergency crash-dive, sealing off the entrances and communicating with no one. I've been there, so have all my friends and colleagues in the business. If you meet a consultant who tells you that he has come through every recession without it having any effect, don't do business with him!

So what do you do when the world you have so carefully created collapses? Well, this sort of thing is as much about psychology as anything else. Here are a few thoughts:

- Never ever tell anyone, outside those of your immediate confidants, that business has just tanked. That is an imperative – THE golden rule.

- Get on with business as usual. Step up your business development time and investment. Your job now is to attract more business. But don't change your attitude, just increase your exposure to clients.

- As long as you believe in what you are doing, be prepared to throw money into the business – isn't that what that six months' survival money (I talked about in Chapter 1) is there for?

- Think and look confident. Although it may seem you are all alone, believe me it has happened to everyone at one time or another.

- Remember that shoulder to cry on. Use it: phone a friend.

- Don't drop your prices or write crazy 'anything-to-get-the business' proposals, you will quickly regret it.

- Launch an initiative that will get you noticed: run a seminar, a survey, an online newsletter (all excuses to contact and talk with your network). Don't hard sell, offer help and advice, it will be appreciated. They may know or suspect you have a few problems, but they will respect you for not crying into your beer.

And what if it stays bad?

- Examine your outgoings. Is there anything you can cut that will save the bottom line? (Sadly, if you are working from home there probably won't be much.) However, with your costs on the floor, any new business coming in flows quickly to the bottom line without getting sucked away by expenses.

- Chase any outstanding debt and push for payment to keep cash-flow as buoyant as possible.

- Go see your bank manager (now you know why you should make him your friend) and check out the options you might have.

- Finally: really push your network hard. Hopefully you'll only have to do this once in every 10 years! Go ask for work. It might be slightly demeaning, but it's a whole lot better than no business at all, or the even worse alternative, getting a REAL job!

Look on the bright side. Hard as it might be, if you have survived as an independent consultant for any length of time, it may take you three to six months to drum up significant new business, but it will come. That can only happen if you really believe in yourself and what you offer. Self-doubts about whether you are any good only generate negative energy.

## THE DAY THE WORLD FELL IN

I've been to the edge of the abyss. In the last 20 plus years there have been three recessions. I survived the first two very well. Recession three was unusual in that every part of the world and most industries went down together. In my case my three biggest billing clients put up the shutters within a month of each other. That tends to concentrate the mind somewhat! Luckily, I had a good cash situation and was able to ride out the storm while seeking new business. It is never easy, it takes a lot of hard work and an ability to face rejection. Sometimes when you see those people with jobs, you feel a little jealous. Until the next time you call up and find that they have been ejected as 'superfluous to requirements'. That's when you realise that the flexibility the independent consultant has is the key to their survival. Certainly I wouldn't want to be anything else.

# Bail-out strategies

Consultants, like everyone else, do get tired and old. Many of them dream of selling out to someone else and enjoying a well-earned retirement. At this stage of life, independent consultants tend to fall into two distinct categories:

> those that want to hang up their keyboards and PowerPoint clickers;

> those that want to just keep on going, doing 'a little bit of this, and a little bit of that'.

For many of those in the first category, the idea of passing on the business to someone else is a possibility. Trouble is that if the business is just YOU, there isn't much to sell. After all, you can hardly leave your brain behind when you close the door for the last time (at least not yet anyway). In observing individuals and small groups trying to cash in on what they have created, I regret to say that most of them have been doomed to disappointment.

In most cases any deal is subject to complex earn-out agreement rules where the seller has to stick around for two, three, four or five years and final compensation is based on the value of the business at that time. And, as I commented above, many individuals will be upset to see how little value is attached to all their life's work.

True, there are always exceptions. Yet even these don't seem entirely satisfactory. One case had the founder pounding the pavements for his soon-to-be American masters, pushing new business as hard as he could (something he had never had to do before). The whole transaction left a bad taste and lost him a lot of respect and credibility in the marketplace.

Frankly, the ones that seem happiest are the good friends that I still work with who have reached their sixties and are still putting in the hours. Not as many hours as before by any means, but they are still very active and very sharp. A lot of these people have forgotten more than a newly minted independent knows, so they are very valuable. They are the elder statesmen of their profession. Called on to provide words of wisdom, get things done and talk a lot at conferences. They still make an income, but they have usually reached that age where money ceases to be the major concern for them. However, they have the time for long lunches with their friends (just like independent consultants did in the heady 1970s and 1980s) and open access to a lot of the great and good. They are useful, often quietly powerful, and with networks to die for. I hope I end up like that one day!

# A final thought

However you decide to develop your business (and only you can make that decision), you have to try and keep that passion and that work culture that you started out with. Get too corporate (too organised, too bureaucratic) and you can lose much of the rationale for what made you become a consultant in the first place. Independent consultants – whatever their specialisation – are a unique breed of people. Most of them are self-motivated and self-regulated. They know how and why things happen and the way they work. They know what it takes to make and sustain success. So before you make major changes, carefully consider what you want to get out of it and what it will do to the business you began. Then, when you have answered that, give yourself a time-frame to make your new plans work. And develop an exit strategy as well, just in case. Sooner or later, the real independent consultant will reassert himself or herself. As I said at the beginning of this book, we are not entrepreneurs. We are consultants who provide a very special and much needed service to the public and private sector. Every day our numbers are growing and will continue to do so. Whatever your plans, wherever you go, the drive and the dream that got your started need to be part of your professional business offering.

# Key learning points

> You don't need to move your business forward. Listen to your own voice, what do you REALLY want?

> If you want to create an alliance or a partnership, try it out for some time before you commit to any legal structure.

> Hiring staff is a huge investment. If there are other ways, try them first.

> Contracting out business works for flexibility, but loyalty and guaranteed availability are not easy to find.

> There's nothing wrong with shrinking the business if you want to develop new interests.

> You need to stay up to date always. Clients expect advice and counsel based on a real awareness of the current climate.

> If you do hire in staff, remember it is YOUR business. Hang on tight to that culture you have created.

> Check out that in all your success you haven't lost focus of why you began the business.

> And when (or if) it all goes wrong, tell a few close confidants and that's all. Never tell the whole world you're in trouble – get on with business as usual.

# Chapter **9**

# Creating YOUR workplace

*'My husband said he needed more space, so I locked him outside.'*

**Roseanne Barr**

YOUR workplace. Doesn't that sound good? For some peculiar reason it's not at all like going to THEIR workplace, where – if you are lucky in these days of open-plan, hot-desking, drop-in 'work pods' – you may have the ultimate luxury, namely your own desk. This is your place. And while it certainly needs to have your personality stamped on it, this tends to grow with time. But whatever it is – and whatever it evolves or mutates into – it is yours and yours alone.

Since I began my independent consultancy career in 1982, I have had a total of five different offices. While I may have had the basic idea of what I needed, after a few months they sort of settled down and developed into a really personal space. Basically, what happened was that they became comfortable like an old shoe. They may have developed a few cracks and lost their shine, but you felt at home in them. So, as you begin to consider life as a solo operator, you need to spend some time thinking through what this 'space' needs to achieve if it is to be effective.

Also remember that for many independents, a large part of their working life may well be spent on the road, meeting customers, working at client locations. While I am yet to be convinced that you can work efficiently in the so-called 'virtual office' where your workspace is anywhere there is a wireless LAN, the overall physical 'footprint' we require has certainly shrunk. If you are the kind of consultant who spends weeks out of an office, but then comes back to toil away on projects, you need to work out just how much space you need and what facilities you need to have at hand. This is going to be your 'home' for up to 12 hours a day, maybe even more, so you had better get to like it.

> **TIP** What you need is somewhere that is efficient and yet makes you feel good. When you have to sit there on a sunny Sunday morning, because a client (who you just know is playing golf) needs something for Monday at 9 o'clock, then you had better have a workplace that attracts you.

For post-industrial man, the independent's workspace becomes the equivalent of yesterday's garden shed. It can provide a haven when other areas of the house suddenly develop into 'no-go' zones. It is also where I keep track of my personal life outside of direct work. So paying bills, leisure Internet surfing and shopping and family travel planning all take place in my space. It is convenient and it works for me. Whether it works for you is a matter of temperament and personal circumstances.

To get you thinking seriously about the workspace issue, I have created a short checklist, which should help you reach some basic conclusions about wants and needs. Remember, you don't have to have it all right away. Just try and make sure that you create a space that can expand over time. After the checklist, I have repeated the questions and added a commentary based on my own experiences.

## CHECKLIST 4: DECIDING ON YOUR WORKSPACE REQUIREMENTS

Getting an early understanding of what your working requirements are going to be will help save costly mistakes later.

| | | |
|---|---|---|
| Can I work from home? | [yes] | [no] |
| Can I have a dedicated area in my home? | [yes] | [no] |
| Will I have clients visiting my home? | [yes] | [no] |
| Will I principally work from my (a) home office, (b) on the road (hotels etc.), or (c) at my client's premises? | [a] [b] | [c] |
| Can I create/do I need an external access to my home office? | [yes] | [no] |
| Do I have enough room to expand, store files, add equipment as I grow the business? | [yes] | [no] |
| Do I have room to create a stand-alone office unit? | [yes] | [no] |
| Do I have room to expand that facility if I need to at a later date? | [yes] | [no] |
| Will there be room for others to work in the space if required? | [yes] | [no] |
| Are there convenient toilet facilities available? | [yes] | [no] |
| Are there alternative office facilities in my town/near my location that I can use? | [yes] | [no] |
| Can I share offices and costs with other professionals? | [yes] | [no] |
| Will I require planning permission to create my office? | [yes] | [no] |

Hopefully, your answers will give you a clearer idea of what is easy to do, what will take some time (and funds), and what you should postpone until you get the business well established (by which time it may be sensible to consider moving your location anyway).

Now let's backtrack and look at these very basic issues again in the light of my own experiences.

## Can I work from home?

I know we touched on this in earlier chapters, but this is the BIG decision. If you have any doubts that you will find it impossible to concentrate on your work (because of young children, elderly relatives or generally noisy environment), then you do need to seek out an alternative. If you simply don't have the space to create your own secure work area, the same applies.

Here's a great test: your best client is on the phone and you are having a four-way conference call that will last an hour. Are you certain you can take that time, take notes and contribute fully in the workspace you are considering you will occupy? Is the dog going to bark at the postman? Is your six-month old daughter going to wake up for her feed? These are the distractions you can't afford to have as a busy, committed professional. For anyone contemplating life as a solo operator, this is the big decision (well the second biggest decision after deciding to go solo). Also your workspace says a lot about you and it needs to reflect who you are if you are to enjoy using the space and be productive.

Yes, I did say ENJOY. This is your space, so you had better really love it.

## Can I have a dedicated work area in my home?

If you've solved problem one and decided that you can work from home (possibly because you are single or your partner goes to a 'real' job every day), the next step is to decide where you are going to work. Personally, I think that wherever you work, it has to be secure in one way or another. Also, if you are working from a house or apartment, it has to be somewhere where you can leave things and go about the rest of your life. It isn't much fun (after the first flush of being an independent has worn off) having to move your entire 'office' because you have friends coming to stay for the weekend and you need the room. Similarly, if you have a partner who works 9 to 5, five days a week, he or she will have to get used to your fledgling independent operator's needs to catch up or prepare at weekends. In my time, I have seen some ingenious mini-workspaces (that make a lot of sense when you are starting out) but they all could be secured and locked away. Face it, you don't want your friends and relations going through your work, or just 'borrowing' a pencil, do you? Neither do you want your children's friends using your notepads as colouring books and the like. Back to those rules again.

## Will I have clients visiting my home?

My view is that if you can keep clients away from your house, do so. If you haven't got some external access or external office (see below), it seems that no time is ever a good time. If they are simply checking you out and you can't avoid it, get it over with quickly and then take them to lunch or something. Many of my clients are friends and over the years we have been to each other's houses (had dinner and so on), but that is a more social affair. That's fine, but if you have restricted work conditions, don't try and do business across the kitchen table while the dog chews the client's shoes and the kids spill juice all over him.

## Can I create an external access to my home office?

If you want to work from home and want a secure space to do it in, think about creating a space that has access from the outside, so clients and suppliers can come and go without disturbing or being aware of the rest of the activity in the house. I have several work colleagues that have done this in a variety of ways and it always makes things look a lot more professional. Look at the following cases:

> An IT consultant reconfigured his original garage (built into the house) and turned that into an office space with a front door from the driveway. It also retained the access door into the rest of the house. He plumbed in a small toilet, so that visiting clients (in his case he had quite a few) didn't have to invade the house at all.

> An independent website creator found an apartment that had a maid's room attached that had external access (and a toilet) to the main staircase. It was small (cosy even) but it provided a great place to start for a small additional rental.

> A young independent marketing communications consultant (his description), otherwise known as a freelance copywriter (my description), turned the basement of the house he rents into a wonderful workspace (excellent for those who don't care about natural light!). The big upside was that it had direct access from the main corridor, making it fully independent from the living quarters.

As with any of these alternatives to 'real' offices, they need to be presentable. While it would perhaps be nice to think that all our clients were as off-the-wall as we are, this is rarely true. So, without being too conservative, make your offices your own, and try not to invite the clients over too often, if at all.

## Planning your stand-alone office unit

When you have some more space available, you are only limited by the level of your imagination. Having a sanctuary where you can work undisturbed is a great boost to any budding independent career. However convenient and cheap it may be to work from inside the four walls of the family home, there is nothing to beat having the freedom that a stand-alone unit can bring.

Recognising the increasing trend for people to work from their home base, manufacturers are coming up with all sorts of offices for the home-worker. While many appear to be little more than one small evolutionary step from the ubiquitous garden shed, others are system-built to totally meet the needs of the twenty-first century solo operator.

If you opt for the the office-in-the-garden type of arrangement, here are a few things you should consider as you plan your professional hide-away.

> What will the neighbours say? People can be difficult (particularly if your cat has a tendency to eat their goldfish), so a good idea (even if you don't need planning permission) is to tell them what you are about to do. Like a lot of other things, a smooth ride in this area works best on the basis of no surprises.

> Get a number of quotes for this dream office. And don't forget to check out local suppliers. I've found them often a whole lot cheaper than the ones you see in the home and garden magazines. If you want ideas of types and prices, try www.hutdesign.co.uk, www.createspace.com and www.aarco.co.uk. All have home offices for the garden or external space from around £5,000 (self

assembly[1]) to over £20,000. If you want something really special (think expensive) try www.oakmasters.co.uk or www.romseyfarm.fsnet.co.uk or www.oakframedirectory.co.uk. My own office was created by a local supplier for 50 per cent of what a national big name wanted to charge me.

➤ Get everything you can plumbed in from the outset. Wiring and piping need to be carefully planned. It is important to get the specification agreed early on, you don't want to have to tear up the floorboards after six months.

➤ Phone lines and broadband connection to the Internet are the mainstay of any modern office. Check first that you can get broadband where you intend to site your office. I know it's fairly ubiquitous, but there are still areas of the country (generally rural ones) where it's not available, in which case you may need to reconsider whether to relocate your office in a nearby town. Remember, you may need to order your broadband well in advance.

➤ Shop around to decide the best supplier for your phone lines/broadband: compare monthly packages and what your specific requirements are in terms of line speed and download capacity (e.g. will you be downloading/sending huge files?).

➤ If you are considering more than one computer in your office, think about installing a wireless hub; your IT adviser or phone company should be able to advise you on this.

➤ Get twice as many electrical sockets as you think you'll need (or count all those you know you will need and multiply by two).

➤ Be careful with the positioning of the office. You don't want to miss out on sunlight, but neither do you want it to blind you or make your computer screen unreadable.

➤ Good lighting is vital, but so is light from windows. Think skylights (with blinds you can lower). You also need a few external lights, so you don't fall down on the way home across the garden. This may sound silly until winter arrives and you haven't done it.

➤ You need adequate ventilation, so make sure windows open easily.

➤ You need to heat and cool most garden offices. The solution is to get an all-purpose air-conditioner that will maintain a basic level of temperature all year round (there are small, highly efficient, wall-mounted domestic units from Samsung, Panasonic, Fujitsu, Toshiba and others, that range from around £1,500 to £2,500

---

[1] Unless you are the DIY king of independent consultants, don't try and do this yourself. Get a professional and pay them to do it properly. This is a tool of your trade, make sure it works to the full. Anyway, while you are trying to construct the damn thing you are not doing your business.

installed). Go to their websites and check them out. If you are considering buying, here are two tips: (a) Get an air-conditioner that is professionally installed and has a service contract deal with it and make sure it is installed when you put up the construction. You don't want them knocking holes in your new office afterwards.

> Put in a toilet facility and hot and cold water (there are plenty of small water heaters that work well). You don't want the disturbance of running across to the house every time nature calls! Also this means if you have clients over, or others working with you, they have the right sort of facilities on site.

> Install a fridge, a kettle and a microwave. This allows you to be fully functional and focused on the task in hand. I also have a nice big couch, great for reading on, which pulls out as a bed. It is also great if you find yourself in the dog house (!) or for those rare times when the entire family comes to stay.

> When it comes to furniture, well there's always IKEA! Seriously, there is nothing wrong with their products for small offices. The other idea is a bespoke office build. Here be careful. I priced out several of these office creators (who advertise in the Sunday newspapers and home magazines) and found them around 50 per cent more expensive than my local carpenter.

> Don't forget maintenance. There's no point in waiting until something goes wrong. Keep it maintained; painting, guttering, wood proofing; check the wiring, heaters etc. And make sure you have an annually maintained set of fire extinguishers.

> Finally, security. Does it have decent locks on doors and windows and is it all insured (including contents such as computers)? You can possibly add it on to your home insurance, but you do need to check this with your insurance provider.

Of course, you don't have to build one of these as a stand-alone, you can always add-on to your home if you have the room. Lots of people I know have added to the rear of garages, built on top of garages or converted existing outbuildings. The important thing is to have a good plan about what you want to do and get that budget set. Unless you are really short of funds, try and get all the basics built in at the time of any conversion.

# Planning permission

There are not many places these days where you can just build what you like. And while most constructors and builders will try to suggest that a small office doesn't need planning permission from the local authorities, don't bet on it. It all depends on where you are located and local regulations. What you need to do is pre-empt any action by checking it out before you go ahead. Having to file for permission retroactively can be costly and time consuming (neither of which you need).

# Do I have room to expand?

When you begin your own consulting firm, it is unlikely you will know where you will be in five years' time, let alone 10. So, where possible, consider carefully the size and accessibility of the office set-up. For example, if you were to have co-workers, would there be room for them or would you have to either build anew or consider renting offices elsewhere? Remember, you don't have to fill all the space, just know that it is there if you need to expand.

Recently, I had an assignment that involved three other key players. Because I had created a sizeable home office, I was able to accommodate all of them comfortably in my rural 'war room'. While this might never happen to you, it is useful to have the space for later expansion or as an 'extra' feature when you sell on.

2 **TIP** When I have intensive work sessions with others at my workplace in the garden, I never let them stay at the house. Reason? If you are putting in 10 or 12 hours of time together (and usually four or five days at a time), everyone appreciates downtime (also it is unfair on your partner/family). What I do is book them into the local public house (200 metres away, with en suite rooms and a killer breakfast) so they have their own space. I am not being unfriendly (often I'll go and have a drink at the end of the day or go for dinner), but when you suggest this arrangement, everyone I've worked with prefers it. No matter how well you get on with work colleagues, we all need downtime.

The other thing about space is that it really does fill up. You are going to create files (that you legally need to keep) and you probably (depending on your business) require storage for publications and an inventory of published materials you use in your business. This all takes up space. In addition, you might add office equipment. A colleague of mine got into terrible trouble when he found himself with an all-singing, all-dancing, state-of-the-art copying machine. To accommodate it he had to entirely redesign his office. The advice on this is: think ahead.

## Are there alternative facilities in town – maybe share the costs with others?

If finding space and working from your own location isn't going to work, or you simply need others around you, then finding a location you can operate from should not be that difficult. These days, even the smallest town – and some villages too – seem to have all sorts of options. It seems that half the farmers in Europe are turning disused cow sheds into office accommodation! Obviously, what you rent or buy is going to depend on the type of business you are starting and the kind of budget you have. But to begin with, think about what you need and what facilities will be required (see our workspace-in-the-garden checklist above). Light and ventilation, plumbed and wired-in services (including IT) are all important.

If you have to meet with clients, is there a meeting room you can reserve? Will my commute be easy? Can I park my car? It is getting the answers to the basics that will determine how useful your new workspace will be.

If you are looking for this type of solution, the next step is to consider whether you can 'bunk-up' with some like-minded independents. This has a lot of advantages. Often there are shared services, everything from IT services to an answer-service or a pooled receptionist, shared kitchen and other physical facilities. In addition to sharing costs, quite a few professionals find the 'social' atmosphere alone a compelling reason to working like this. They say that being able to share ideas as well as high and lows with others is a huge advantage. Others just need to be out of the home environment in their professional life.

If you decide to go down this route, it is crucial to get the deal in writing, so you know exactly what you are buying into. Failure to do that can result in all sorts of hidden charges and costs. And it is not only important to know the costs on your way in. You need to be fully aware of what it will cost to get OUT too.

# Fixing up the facilities

In creating an external office, there are a few must-haves like air-conditioning and good lighting. This is just as true for an office inside your home. What you want is a pleasant working environment that lets you perform to your very best. So check them out, you will be glad you did.

# Play safe

Go out and buy a safe. Crazy? OK, you haven't got the Crown Jewels in your office – you've got something more important – your professional life. Lose all that and where are you? A decent safe is not that expensive. What you need is one that is (a) fireproof and (b) heavy enough to give two burglars a guaranteed hernia trying to lift it. My safe (I've had it for 20 years) contains:

- the articles of incorporation of the company (a copy is also filed with my law firm and my accountant);
- hard copy file of current invoices;
- hard copy file of recent proposals;
- hard copy file of contract agreements;
- cheque books and related banking documents;
- credit card numbers and various access codes;
- credit cards, hotel and airline loyalty cards that I use only when travelling;
- foreign currency (US dollars, Euros, Swiss francs etc.,) to pay taxi fares if necessary;
- passports (the whole family), plus birth, marriage and other certificates;
- contracts and claim forms for travel insurance, medical cover etc.;
- CDs that back-up my computer and copies of key manuscripts (books, research projects etc.).

A functional safe is not expensive. You can buy one that will store what I have listed above for less than £300 (€450) and one of those hotel-type digi-safes that you can have cemented or cut into the wall in a discreet place for under £150 (€200). That's a small price to pay for peace of mind.

# Does it have a view?

This may sound silly to some – it's not. It is all about how you orientate your workspace. Why put yourself facing a blank wall if you can position your desk so that you can see out of a window (any window will do). I believe that being able to see a patch of sky or the other side of the street lets you know there is a world out there. On some days, when things are not going too well, it helps – really!

## MY SPACE – FROM HELL TO HEAVEN

Five years ago, I was able to create my own workspace from the ground up – literally. Finding a house you love and being able to live in it is a dream for many. We found that. The added bonus was an old artist's studio (like a small Victorian cricket pavilion) with huge north-facing windows. Trouble was it was ready to fall down! After paying to have what I thought was going to be my new office taken down, I was left with a large 'footprint' to create a new workspace from the ground up.

One of the early lessons I learned was to think BIG. It doesn't really cost a great deal more (once you are signed up to build) to add extra space to the project. What I now occupy as working space is about the length and breadth of a static caravan – except this is an oak-framed, timbered construction, roofed with reclaimed antique tiles. There is enough room inside for four or five desks if ever it was necessary, plus space for visitors. At the rear is a toilet and shower.

The concept I came up with was one that allows me to expand if required (without any additional capital outlay), but it also fulfils two other needs. First, I deliberately planned it as a multiple-use build-ing. It could be transformed at very little cost into a granny/guest apartment, games/billiard room etc. (all the facilities for that are either installed or were plumbed/wired into the frame at construc-tion). This has added hugely to the value of the whole property, making it especially interesting to anyone wanting to start or develop a business. This is important. Chances are you won't stay in your current location for ever, so making your workspace not just attrac-tive to you but desirable to others (no matter what they eventually use it for) is a great boost for the business and your pocket.

While I appreciate only too well that not everyone has the room to do this to this extent, keep your eyes very wide open. Instead of creating that super garden shed style, is there another way? Could you get permission for two storeys? Could you dig down and create a basement and ground floor? Finally, don't be limited by what you see in catalogues. As I said earlier, I had a local builder put my office together for approximately 50 per cent less than the cost in the fancy catalogues and magazines. It pays to shop around.

## '... with one enormous chair'

To paraphrase from the song 'Wouldn't it be Luverly' from the musical *My Fair Lady*, all I want is that one enormous chair. You see, you can't sit at a desk staring at a VDU all day ... and possibly all night too. What you need are two things, stretch breaks (to postpone the day your body locks itself into a permanent stoop) and a big comfy chair and a footstool. With that you can read papers, take breaks and generally be a little more civilised than the rest of toiling humanity may think you are. So when planning your workspace, try to allow enough room for that chair too.

Also, don't forget that this is YOUR space, not THEIRS. You are no longer an employee, therefore you can do what you want. There is something really great about cranking up the music on a rainy February day (you can't do that in an open plan office environment, can you?) and getting on with your work. Yes, when you get that first assignment, celebrate and go out and buy a really good music centre.

## Where do all those office supplies come from?

If you have only worked in a corporate environment up to now, there's a good chance you won't know the answer to this one. Why should you? You never needed to know before. You had heard rumours of a big cupboard somewhere, but that was all. Basically, it sort of arrived when you needed it. Now you are on your own. So how do you go about buying all those accessories for your office? Basically, you have two options:

> ➤ If you plan to use a lot of materials, set up an account with an office supply firm and get it delivered. They should also give you a discount if you order enough from them.

> ➤ If you are not at all sure how much you'll need, go and buy some basics and then work it out as you use it.

> **3** **TIP** WARNING! People who have never been into an office supply superstore need to be accompanied by a responsible adult. You don't need all those multi-coloured paper-clips even if they are on offer – honest!

In my own case, I use a lot of paper and a lot of ink and frankly that's about it. So, what I do is to bulk-buy these items and then once a year buy the rest on one trip to a big discount store. And despite being careful, I'll never use all those colourful paper-clips either!

So, what do you need to stock a basic independent consultant's office with what used to be called stationery and supplies? Here's a list:

| | |
|---|---|
| Printer paper | Rolodex and inserts (optional) |
| Notepads | Burnable CDs |
| Post-it Notes (several colours) and sizes | Blank diskettes |
| Envelopes: several sizes | In and Out type trays |
| Envelopes: padded | Message/noticeboard and pins |
| Envelopes for CD/diskettes | Paper adhesive |
| Mailing tubes for large items | Scissors |
| Plastic folders | Letter-opener |
| Box files | Document punch |
| Stapler and staples | Document binder machine (optional) |
| Paper clips | and materials |
| Bulldog clips | Letterheads |
| Pens: several types and colours | Business Cards |
| Pencils | Compliments cards |
| Eraser(s) | Desk diary |
| Marker Pens | Wall planner (optional) |
| Ruler, measuring tape | Reference materials: |
| Calculator for desk (large numbers) | Dictionary |
| Calculator for pocket | Thesaurus |
| Scotch tape dispenser and tape | World Atlas |
| Adhesive type for wrapping materials | Local/national atlas/maps |
| | Transport timetables |

# Back to THOSE rules

Now we have an office and some workspace. What else do we need? RULES for a start! You will recall that I have already laid down the law on this in Chapter 2. However, I really don't think that this can be said enough: make sure you have rules for your workspace and that they work for you – no one else.

While you are not exactly in prison (although it can feel like that some days), you need to let those around you know when they have visiting rights. Basically my work area is mine unless I agree otherwise. And I keep it that way.

Despite that, things DO happen:

> ➤ Beware of clutter-creep. Things appear, because your office becomes a storeroom for stuff that others don't know what to do with.

> ➤ Because you own all the Scotch-tape, scissors etc., it is convenient to use your office as a 'wrapping room'.

> ➤ It becomes the convenient hidey-hole. Last Christmas all the presents ended up on my spare desk, plus those for the school Christmas party.

> ➤ Don't install a large fridge. I made the mistake of putting our upright fridge freezer in the back of the office. This creates opportunities for multiple visits.

> ➤ Learn to dread – and be politically deaf to – the phrase, 'just put this in your office dear for a day or two.' Things seem to take up permanent residence.

Also make sure that people don't just drop in. My son (who is 7 years old) knows that he can't just drop by. By creating rules and sticking with them, everyone soon gets the message and it is much better all round.

# The challenge of staying connected

While we have covered a lot of the detail of staying in touch in earlier chapters, what we haven't yet tackled is how to keep ourselves in front of our clients. It really doesn't matter what you choose as a method of staying in touch with your clients as long as (a) they can reach you when they need to and (b) everything you have on the IT side is compatible with theirs.

We all know that technology is turning phones into computers and vice versa. Our need to be in a fixed place to have a conversation or pass notes and images to each other has vanished. All the same, you are going to have to invest in one or two expensive basics to get you going.

So for most offices today we are talking about:

> a main computer (although you could use a lap-top with a docking station);
> a lap-top (or a combi with a mobile phone);
> a fixed line phone (with two lines and broadband);
> a mobile phone or blackberry-type device;
> a printer;
> a scanner;
> a fax.

There are multi-choices in the technology you need. What matters is how well it works for you. You can get into all sorts of discussions on this, but the easy way is to work backwards. Don't look at the hardware. Ask yourself, 'What do I need it for?' then find what fits best.

Let's use what I work with as an example:

> I have a **main computer** (we have a total of two in a WiFi local area network LAN). I tend to keep these up to date and have my IT consultant give them a good clean-out once or twice a year.
> I have a **lap-top** that is fast, tough, very light, with a long battery life and a great keyboard. On lap-tops, I find the better the features the more you pay (weight and battery-life being premiums).
> My **fixed line phone** has two lines, plus my broadband (there is a fax line too, but linked onto the broadband line). I suppose that soon we won't need fixed lines and will be able to make do with mobiles. Right now I am waiting.

**TIP** Every independent consultant needs at least two lines. You need to be able to answer while you are on the phone to another customer.

> A **mobile phone** with good e-mail facilities. This means that on short trips (a day or two) I don't need to take my lap-top. Equally, the mobile has to be able to go for two days without a recharge. Although if you are smart, you'll know where to sneakily plug in your charger at restaurants and other public places. I have not embraced messaging as much as I possibly should. I'd still rather pick up a phone and talk than use e-mail. Face it, consultants are supposed to talk to people.

> **Printer and scanner**, fairly basic, but they do the job. I have never been comfortable with those combination fax/printer/scanner machines. One part of the technology always seems to be woefully inadequate.

> My **fax** I am convinced is obsolete, until the one time every month I need it. Recently, with e-mails getting lost a lot more (the way faxes used to), I have noticed a little more traffic. Today, faxes get attention, e-mails don't. So I'm not going to throw it away – yet.

> **Answering** and **call divert**, are two life-lines, without which the independent consultant would have to pay someone to do the job. Call divert is my main feature, allowing me to be 'in the office' wherever I am in the world. As I said earlier, for longer trips I use an answering service.

## Staying ahead

The key to technology for me is to update it when you see either very real gain or a danger in falling behind the applications your clients use. The very real gain has to make something, easier and quicker or you more accessible. Playing catch-up is just one of the investments you know you'll have to keep making. Personally, I think it is better to try and keep up incrementally than make big technical leaps. Somehow, those that do never seem to catch up with the rest of us.

When you consider what the last 20 years have brought in technology to the workplace, you have to be a little scared about what the next 20 will bring. Sitting here with my wireless keyboard and mouse, staring at my giant flat screen, with my broadband connection linking me to just about anything I want, it is easy to think you have the ultimate. But I know that more technologies are going to change that (I've already witnessed some at first hand). The image revolution is next, already I am having live/on-screen conversations. This will really take off as soon as our clients seriously adopt it and we have to follow. How I am going to get around the fact that I am still at lunch (even if it is with another client) at 4 o'clock on a Friday I just don't know. Is this where technology ceases to be fun?

What, for me, is one of the biggest issues today is the assumption by others that technology works, when we know it is fallible. Too often these days, personal assistants send e-mails to cancel or re-arrange meetings when you are not in a position to pick it up. Or it simply never gets to you.

**5** **TIP** I make a point of re-confirming every meeting or appointment 24 hours before the event. In today's disorganised world it is a good discipline to have.

For the independent consultant, being in touch is vital. Years ago we had assistants or secretaries, today we tend to be on our own, because the technology has made it possible. But think, until someone comes up with time travel, we can't be in two places at the same time. Technology will help us get, carry out and deliver the business, but it isn't the driver. It is only a very useful assistant to those of us who know how to use it properly and be unsurprised by its failings. There are too many would-be solo operators who don't fully realise that. No amount of technology will sell anything for you. It is YOU that people are buying. Sure they expect you to stay in touch, but it is your ideas, your energy and enthusiasm that will be the deciding factor whether you get the business or not.

## Get professional help

In all this, make certain you have access to professional help. No matter how good the gadgets and gizmos are today, a lot of them don't do quite what it says on the box. The professionals know (well they should know) what bits work best with what. They also know how to help in a crisis. So, make sure you have easy, face-to-face access with a knowledgeable IT expert. And remember, you will pay for what you get and YES, it can be too cheap! None of us today can afford our systems to be down for very long. We depend on them too much for that. You are operating a professional service and charging professional fees. So when you need help, use professionals too.

## Key learning points

> Can you work from home or close by? If you can great, it keeps down costs and commuting time.

> You must have a dedicated area in your home that is safe, secure and where you can work undisturbed.

> Try and have an external access to your office. It is better for deliveries, visiting clients and creating an climate of professionalism.

> If you are going to build a workspace in your garden, check it out with the neighbours and make sure you don't need official permission.

> Put in a toilet facility and running water and be able to heat and cool the property.

> Make sure you have room to expand if the business grows or for storage space.

> If home alone isn't for you, are there nearby office facilities that you can rent or share with other professionals?

> Don't regret it later, buy a safe and make sure it is fireproof and heavy.

> Get comfy! Apart from a good desk chair, you need a nice big upholstered chair to do your thinking in.

> Be careful with office supplies; you can buy too much – easily!

> You are the office, you have to stay connected wherever you are.

> Just because you are on your own doesn't mean you can stop learning – keep as up to date as you can, and that goes for your equipment too.

# Chapter **10**

# The travelling independent consultant

*'He who would travel happily must travel light.'*

**Antoine de Saint-Exupéry**

*'Travelling may be one of two things – an experience we shall always remember, or an experience, which alas, we shall never forget.'*

**Rabbi Julius Gordon**

Consultants were born to travel. Unless you are very lucky (although I personally like travelling), as an independent, you will be on the move for a large part of your professional time. That is how business gets secured, carried out and delivered. You may travel around your region, around the country, across Europe or all over the globe. Whatever happens, it is useful to set some standards: always knowing that the client's own travel policies may occasionally prevail over your preferences.

## Getting prepared

Do you remember that song 'I Don't Like Mondays', well I know – I think we all know – how Bob Geldof felt. Monday is never a great day, and down through history everyone from Churchill and Stalin (reputedly) to the cartoon cat Garfield have loathed it. If you are a traveller there is a good reason for that – it is NOT the day to go away. Why? Because everyone else wants to. Motorways are clogged, train platforms packed and airports consist of queues and more queues.

Consequently, as I have got older (and maybe just a little wiser), I have begun to travel on a Sunday. What this does for me is get me into a hotel at my Monday work location early to late evening. I get myself fully organised for the next day and I AM THERE. Too many times, I have faced the crush of an airport or rail station on a Monday only to be delayed by bad weather or some other excuse. The end result is that you arrive at your client late and your entire schedule is ruined. This does not send good signals out to your client about your professionalism. So, even if it costs me (i.e. I pay the hotel night), I do it. That way I am always there and rested and effective.

Now there may well be good reasons for not giving up part of your Sunday, but if you can, try it. It makes a lot of sense.

The other thing NOT to do, is come home Friday evening. Why? Because everyone else (or at least all those who haven't read this book) is on the road, in the train, on the plane. The worst place to be on a Friday night is a major airport or rail station. People just want to get home and don't mind how many toes they tread on doing it. If you can come home Thursday, or Friday morning, it is a totally different travel experience.

As for preparation, I never (unless it is forced on me by circumstance) pack at the last minute. If I am leaving on a Sunday afternoon, I will get all my paperwork and technology (the lap-top and attendant bits and pieces) ready Friday at the end of the working day. Then I know where everything is. While this may sound a little nerdy to some, it works for me and I always know where everything is and feel I am properly prepared.

> **1** **TIP** I always travel with duplicate cables for Internet links, for the reason that I once got one stuck in a hotel room outlet and could not get it out without breaking it. Also duplicate phone chargers make sense too, not forgetting travel plug adapters. To make sure I never forget anything, I have a plastic zip-lock bag with everything permanently packed inside. All I need to do is pick it up and put it in my bag.

## Travelling light

Let's face it, unless we are a movie star, it is inconvenient to take a lot of luggage. In fact what we want to do (and the airlines in particular conspire continuously against us) is be able to keep our bag with us at all times. Whether you can achieve that or not depends very much on your ability to pare down what you bring with you. The travel rule has come to be minimise, minimise and then minimise some more.

However, be careful. Except for day trips – and an occasional overnight where I know what I will be doing – I always take a spare pair of trousers (when someone has spilt melted butter on your only pair of pants on the first evening of a two-day trip you learn!), they have come in handy lots of times.

What you need to achieve as a consultant is a sense of understated elegance and organisation, without ending up hauling a huge bag. If I travel in a jacket and slacks, I only need the one pair of shoes and the topcoat goes with both jacket and suit. I can add a tie to the shirt when I put on the suit and take it off in the evening.

I also have a miniature toilet bag (a tiny leather thing I got given by an airline about 20 years ago that seems to never wear out). I continually seek out anything in the way of toiletries that is small (most manufacturers haven't a clue about this and could make a fortune if they tried a little harder). My toilet bag never gets emptied, just refilled, so it is always ready to drop into my travel gear at a moment's notice.

## Luggage planning

It's a good idea to invest in some decent luggage for two reasons:

1 It will last longer and probably have the features you need.
2 Your client won't think that he is the only business you have and therefore try to cut your fees – again!

I have five pieces of luggage I can call on depending on the circumstances of the travel:

1 For day trips I have a computer bag (the one with double shoulder straps in case I am carrying a lot).

2 For more formal day trips (and up to three-day trips), I have a leather bag that has expanding sides as well as a matching small lap-top bag that fits inside. The way it is laid out I can get all my papers in one part and all my personal items in the other (many of my independent peers find what are known as airline pilot's cases a useful equivalent). It has a padded shoulder strap and works well and looks better and better the older it gets.

3 A hard-shell small wheeled case that fits into overhead bins (when security allows it these days!). This is ideal for two or three days away.

4 I have a suit-bag (on wheels). This is like those little wheelie-cases that should go in overhead lockers but never do. Except this will keep suits and jackets in a well-pressed condition, and has an expansion area so I can put my topcoat in there too. I have also reached the stage where I check in items, and keep the critical stuff (including my miniaturised toilet bag) with me in my leather bag. That way, if my bag gets lost (which in truth has only happened once in the last five years) I have a fresh shirt etc., so I can go see clients without any problems. And YES, I always carry my lap-top with me.

5 A monster, all-wheel Samsonite. This is the 'off-road', 4 x 4, mother of all suitcases and comes out only for the big events where lots of clothes and work materials are needed.

## Travelling with clients

Over the years, I must have read a zillion words about management and doing business. Never in all that time have I read anything about one of the toughest assignments you can ever get as a consultant – travelling with your client. I mean, so conscious are we today about ourselves that even the venerated journal the *Harvard Business Review* has begun featuring in-depth *Managing Yourself* articles. But nowhere is there any mention of one of life's most challenging moments – sharing a train, plane or automobile with your client (they don't even do it for the boss – subordinate relationship). But believe me, long-term, close proximity to a client is really hard work.

To give you an idea of what is involved, it is similar to going on vacation for the first (and only) time with your best friend and discovering that they just aren't the same person once they have stepped on that plane. The same applies entirely to your client, only perhaps more so, in that there are not a lot of things you can do about it – except quit.

In the course of my professional career as an independent consultant, I have been to conferences, trade shows and road shows with clients. And I have watched in horror as these people change, like in one of those cheap horror movies.

For some it is party, party, party. For others it is girls, girls, girls. Others still, gamble, gamble, gamble. I have lost count of all the mild-mannered Clark Kents I have chaperoned over the years, except they don't turn into Superman, but one of his evil enemies instead. Then you get back home and the first day you visit the client after the horrors of the trade-show or whatever, it's as if nothing ever happened. My advice to you is to go along with it: nothing ever happened!

Also you'll find that most often they want you to lead them along, find the taxis and the places you are due to visit. So even if they are nursing the world's greatest hangover, you don't want to be in the same state as they are. My trick, honed to a fine art over thousands of unwanted late-night sessions, is to VANISH. I will appear to be headed for the men's room and I just don't come back. I go to bed and stay there. When it gets to bail-out time, everyone else is too preoccupied or, frankly, beyond rational thought, to remember when you packed it in. If there is anyone rankled that you are fighting fit and ready to go the following day, they will soon appreciate your ability to get things organised.

Having said that, I have had many great times on tour with clients. But it isn't always people who you would naturally make friends with in private life. Professional commitments throw all sorts of people together. You need to make certain you can get some downtime and escape to your hotel room to decompress. Believe me, it is necessary.

# Travel rules for independents

Whether you are travelling around your own country or across the world for your job, some basic rules do seem to apply. Most of these we pick up by bitter experience as we develop our businesses. Others are simple, common sense.

My number one rule is that I always travel the day before a critical meeting. And as I have said earlier, Sunday evenings are a far more civilised time to travel than the mania of a Monday morning. In my early days working on my own, I recall the regular horror of realising that there was a delay caused by 'something' that meant I wouldn't make that critical meeting (and therefore, none of the others I had built around it either).

Yes, it will cost a little more, but I have found that clients appreciate people who show up on time. It makes you look that much more professional and creates a feeling that you can be relied on. Also, when you have time in your hotel room you can get a lot of things done. Or, as many of my friends do, just unwind for a few hours. As many of them, who have busy professional and private lives, say 'you have no idea how much I appreciate a few hours on my own.'

### WHAT TIME, WHICH CITY?

This is a very important tip for anyone who has an international portfolio to juggle. Make sure that anyone who helps you realises that the world is broken down into time zones! Assistants get it wrong all the time. If you have any doubts there is a great website www.time anddate.com. What it allows you to do is input the name of your location and it works out actual times against other global locations. This is terrific if you have to arrange a conference call between Memphis, Manchester and Mumbai, as it will show you optimum times to do it (i.e. usual working hours).

# Getting the best deals

Independent professionals are some of the most sinned-against travellers. In fact we probably keep the airlines and hotel chains in business. Big corporate clients get travel deals that we poor solo workers can only dream of. So it means that we need to consider carefully how we book our travel. I live in the hope that someone will open a really good site for independents – the ones that exist are not all that good and their services seem very hit-or-miss.

If we have a good relationship with our clients, we can always ask them to book us into hotels at their rate. This can save you anything from 25–50 per cent on what you might pay as a solo operator. The same goes for air travel. Many of my own clients have automatic upgrades from full-fare economy to business for long-haul travel. So it does pay to ask.

The other thing to do is find hotels that you like and do deals with them. Usually if you can commit to between 15 and 20 days each year, they'll be happy to discount your room (often to a significant degree). Find a good hotel in an area you like and then ask for a meeting with the manager. If the manager is any good, they'll know who you are and be happy to do a deal.

If you are going to be in a city for a good number of days a year, you want a place to stay that gives you some home comforts and some feeling of a 'home-away-from-home' each time you arrive.

In choosing hotels (unless my client is kind enough to help me out), I look for a series of things:

> easy transport access;
> good lobby, informal areas for meetings;
> room with a working desk;
> a quiet room location at the back (I don't care about the view if there's a major street outside);
> room service;
> fast laundry facility;
> low turnover of staff (so they know you and you know them);
> a 'neighbourhood' location, where you can find small restaurants and bars (and breakfast) and newspapers to avoid exorbitant hotel dining 'experiences'.[1]
> a fridge that you can actually put things into – for snacks etc. (again avoiding room service).

The other thing I do – for those moments when I want to switch off from work and don't want to read, is carry a few favourite DVDs with me, so I can watch them on my lap-top. It avoids being charged for in-room movies by the hotel, also it is really useful if your plane is delayed or even during the actual travel 'experience', as the advertisements call it.

Now this may add a little to your travel budget, but don't downmarket yourself too much. Cheap hotels are rarely that cheap. If you shun the five-star 'palaces' and check out carefully three- and four-star, you'll soon find a place that you like, that is very liveable in. Often, after I have 'discovered' these places my clients choose to use them too. However, remember that it has to be a place where you can meet your clients and prospects without you looking like a down-at-heel shoe salesman. So choice is vital, it says a lot about you.

And don't forget that a host of Internet sites offer great deals too. I have become a serial user of sites like www.laterooms.com and www.expedia.com because they offer such great deals for the independent consultant. I was delighted recently when I met an old friend in the lobby of a seriously expensive five-star hotel to discover that my late-room deal was 50 per cent cheaper than his organisation's corporate rate!

[1] In any major city in Europe a good-quality hotel charges £15 (€20) and upwards for breakfast. In London, Paris, Brussels, Amsterdam and Zurich I have friendly cafés two minutes' walk from my regular hotels where I can eat better for less than £5 (€7.50); and they are a lot more fun!

## To book or not to book?

It is strange to think that a few years ago I wouldn't be (couldn't be) writing this section at all. Yet such has been the enormous take-up of the Internet that many independents have eschewed their travel agents and moved on to do it themselves.

Certainly, after decades of dealing with a travel agent (and spending upwards of £25,000 a year with them), I haven't used one in the last three years. Why?

> They charge around £20 (€30) per ticket they issue.

> I can – and have – found cheaper deals than the ones they offer.

The only time this isn't true (and this is already changing as I write) is for multiple destination trips and interlining (using more than one airline). Of course, it does take time to do the research, but as most consultants tend to go back to specific places (at least for the period of a contract or assignment), once the basics are plugged into your 'favourites', it takes just minutes to make a reservation the second and subsequent times.

## Welcome to the throw-away society

With online booking so prevalent, I have also discovered that it is better to 'buy' really cheap, non-refundable tickets and take the chance on something in your plans changing rather than paying the premium for fully flexible tickets. For most airlines and other travel operators, the difference is usually around 50 per cent. For those of us who travel considerably, having to throw away the odd reservation still makes our travel much, much cheaper than a few years ago. This means that any independent consultant can afford to prospect a lot more broadly than before.

There is, as always in these things, a downside. Today, most of us end up in the back of the bus – but then so do most employees (on short haul at least). The only time I insist on being upfront is on long trips. However, the advent of Premium Economy on a lot of long-haul airlines has done much for those of us who are tall.

It is the same with hotels. You don't book yourself into five-star hotels (unless your client has a rate), so, as I pointed out earlier, finding those small, comfortable hotels is vital.

> **2** **TIP** Just as with hotels, cheap options on local travel can turn out expensive. If I am spending a lot of time in one place, I usually locate a car and driver, because at the end of the day, they cost little more than a dirty taxi. It also means you don't queue at airports and you can plan your out-of-town client visits meticulously. Also if you are travelling with clients, they will appreciate your knowledge of the place you are visiting.

## Charging travel time

I know of very few independent consultants who charge travel time 'upfront'. But, it usually gets built into proposals one way or another. However, if a client sends you off around a series of towns or cities, then they should be paying for the block of time they are taking up. The same applies to expenses. I charge travel expenses when I am travelling for a client, but not to go and see them if I am in a different location from them. As I indicated earlier in discussing development costs, the smart independent consultant needs to know how to 'massage' these kind of costs into the overall assignment. Sadly, some will for ever remain 'sunk' costs; this is the price of doing business today.

> **3** **TIP** Unless I have no option but to get into a location and out again, I will always try and see at least one other 'contact' whenever I travel. First, it keeps up – or adds to – your network. Second, you just might get lucky. Strangely enough, I have often picked up business for the sole reason that I was the person in a prospective client's office when an assignment cropped up.

## Expenses on the road

I imagine that everyone has their own rules for keeping track of expenses on the road. Mine are very simple. I only ever use American Express for business travel (with a MasterCard back-up for those annoying places where they refuse Amex!). Any cash transactions are paid with my own money and expensed to the business on my return.

In an age that boasts instant access to credit cards, my choice of Amex as a business card is simple:

> They are very efficient.

> They have a great award programme (and the points don't expire).

> If you have a Platinum card, their travel insurance is exemplary.

> They have a card that gets you (and anyone with you) free access into airline lounges (priceless!).

> If you clear your charges every month you have unlimited credit (necessary for travel).

As with everything else in an independent's existence, you have to seek out the things that work for you in your situation. But by keeping business costs and personal costs separate, you won't spend hours trying to work out which is which. It is a simple thing, but like a lot of this stuff, it is the simple things that work well and often only come after some trial and error.

That, for example, is why I usually insist on buying my own tickets – unless a client has a steal of a deal. First, it means that you are always flexible and can change your travel plans up to the very last minute (something many independents have to do). Second, you can rack up those points – which do come in useful.

## BEWARE THE GEOGRAPHICALLY CHALLENGED

If you do use external help or get busy enough to hire a part-time or full-time assistant, make sure that they understand that there is a big world out there that has different times and other stuff like that, including places with similar names.

Two events that happened to me illustrate this:

> I was in Tokyo, jet-lagged, but had finally fallen asleep when there was a whirring noise fairly close to my ear. I was convinced there was some huge, lethal insect about to attack. Flinging off the covers, I grabbed a shoe and chased around the room. Only to discover neatly tucked away in a cupboard a fax machine, to which my new assistant back in Europe was sending a message. For me it was almost midnight, for her it was four in the afternoon!

> I had recruited a young, enthusiastic graduate who had excelled in everything I gave him to do. Part as reward and part as further training, I sent him off to meet with one of my clients in the US. We flew together to London, where he was

to board his transatlantic flight. As a novice global trekker, he asked me to look at his ticket to work out which terminal in Heathrow he was to leave from. Lucky he did. He was supposed to be going to Portland, Maine, via Boston. He had a ticket for Portland, Oregon via Seattle. Our new assistant had done it again!

## Staying in touch on the road

Being 'available' is one of the most critical aspects of the independent consultant's life. You can possibly get away with being relaxed about other aspects of the business, but being reachable is set in stone. It is the very foundation of our existence. Getting a reputation for being difficult or (God forbid) impossible to reach is a death-knell. So, yes, mobile phones and blackberries are a life-line, especially if they are compatible with your lap-top.

Having said that, don't think I am suggesting that you never switch off. On the contrary. But just make sure that you have surrounded yourself with the people and technology that make it possible for you to respond to five-alarm fires from your palm-fringed beach in the Caribbean. Oh and another thing. If you are in the middle of nowhere, when you arrive, find out just how easy it is (or isn't) to get out of there in an emergency. Too few people think this one through until it is too late. For example, would you go on vacation to some location where there are only two or three flights a week? You would? Wrong answer!

As I pointed out earlier in the book, call diverts, message services and mail diverts are all available – there's just no excuse these days to be 'missing and out of the action'.

## The workplace is where you lay your lap-top

Much as I love my office, I am totally at home working from virtually any-where. This is based on my early days as a journalist where you had to write and call in stories in all sorts of situations and strange locations. So, no matter where I am, I can usually find a calm, quiet spot (and I make a point of remembering them) where I can either work, or just turn off for a few hours if I have to.

There is no doubt that today the workplace IS everywhere. From my own experiences, here is my take on some of them.

### The workplace is everywhere no. 1: the airline lounge

Virtually all the solo consultants I know are as at home in an airline lounge as anywhere else. Incidentally, it is definitely worthwhile having access to lounges (the service that American Express accords me – access to Priority Pass affiliated lounges – is excellent because it doesn't depend on which airline you are flying). Most lounge access gets restricted to which level of traveller the airline considers you to be. Which means that if you suddenly find yourself on 10 return trips to Edinburgh, you never build up enough equity in the so-called frequent flyer programme of that airline to get access to anything. Then, just as your client's assignment is over, the airline sends you a card that gives you lounge access in an airport you will probably never go to again! What you need is a lounge pass that will get you away from the crowds virtually anywhere around the globe. Your family will thank you for this too when they travel along.

I have hung out in airport lounges in snowstorms and strikes. And although they can get a bit crowded at peak travel times, they can offer a quiet place to sit and work. Also, I have made it my business to find a little oasis of calm in all the airports I regularly use. There are always some, even on the busiest day in the summer, where you can squirrel yourself away and ignore the rest of seething humanity.

> **TIP** All the good 'corners' I know also have wall sockets, which means you can recharge your lap-top and mobile phone. This is especially handy if you are delayed for a while.

### The workplace is everywhere no. 2: the hotel lobby

One highly successful independent management consultant I know does not have an office: never has, never will. His entire working life – in which he meets hundreds of people – takes place in the lobbies of Europe's most business-friendly hotels. Please note the 'business-friendly' tag, for this is important.

What you need are hotel lobbies where you can have a discreet discussion, order breakfast, coffees, light lunches, tea and the odd glass of wine, without any eyebrows being raised. Sure these 'friendly' locations occasionally disappoint (usually new management), but there are some that have given him and myself hundreds of hours of good service.

In some cases it might be a place you stay, but most of the time, it is a location that the person you are meeting can easily find: indeed, they will probably be impressed by your choice of venue. When you consider that most of us meet one-on-one or in fairly small groups (three to four), renting meeting rooms is a chore and costs money. The whole idea is to keep costs down (that other watchword of the successful independent operator) and this is a great, totally professional way to do it.

Clubs and professional associations can offer similar facilities, but so many of them frown on the active process of a business discussion that they usually ban any papers or other indications of commercial activity taking place. This is no good. They also tend to ban mobile phones.

Most important for this sort of thing to be successful is to look like you belong. Confidence is of the essence. And as long as you buy the occasional breakfast and the odd glass of wine for your 'guests', the smart hotelier will leave you to get on with your business. If you're smart, you will also make sure that you are welcomed. The right sort of tips to the right people working the lobby and the front door do not go amiss or unnoticed.

> **5** **TIP** Make sure you stake your claim to a prime space early; after the morning tourist rush is best.

Don't forget that the hotel is also a source of other 'services'. You can have courier deliveries sent there (well, you could be checking in) if you are travelling, and you can order taxis (especially useful when it is raining).

## The workplace is everywhere no. 3: public places

Increasingly we live in a comfort-obsessed society and so more and more 'spaces' are open for the use of travelling people. Recently, I have been compiling a list of art galleries, museums and other public spaces that have seating areas and food and drink available too (many also have free Internet connections and wireless LAN). Again, begin to compile a list of places. You will be surprised just how many are perfect for interviews and discussions with clients.

## The workplace is everywhere no. 4: restaurants

'Doing lunch' can often be a major part of the independent consultant's mating dance. But again, what you want is a place that impresses your contact (without depressing your bank account) and makes him or her feel at ease. I patronise a regular set of places where I am known well enough to get that slightly better table. There are two sure-fire ways to do this:

> ➤ Get there early (use the time to pre-brief yourself) and just ask for a bigger, or more discreet table.

> ➤ Be really naughty and book a table for three (when there are only two of you).

What I look for in a restaurant is a place with tables well spaced so your conversation doesn't spill into the next group (bistros are not good places to meet for business as you never know who is at the next table). My favourites are eating places with booths, where you can settle in for a long session and ignore the rest of the world.

## The workplace is everywhere no. 5: OPOs (Other People's Offices)

Why so few people think of this I don't know. OPOs are THE very best really, but they only work if you have put that hard work into developing your network. I have a host of non-competing independent consultants who are only too delighted to let me borrow an office, even for a meeting with one of my clients. As long as the offices don't look like they are about to be condemned by a building surveyor, they can help to enhance a client relationship. The client realises that you 'know' people and this is usually deemed to be a 'good thing'. Similarly, your kind friend who has loaned you a meeting room or whatever hopefully thinks that this may be an opportunity for them too. Free office coffee never tasted so good!

## The workplace is everywhere no. 6: restrooms

Finally one place that most people may never consider, but is truly fantastic, offering privacy, security and a spotless environment in which to work – the rest rooms of very good hotels! Over the years, I have carefully kept a note of the best loos in most cities in Europe (and quite a few in the US too). These are rest rooms that are not fully manned, so they don't see you go in. But they are the ones that get cleaned every 30 or 60 minutes (there's always a checklist on the back of the entrance door to prove it). Large stalls, fully air-conditioned, a hook to hang your coat, good locations also have a window-ledge or other place to put your bag. Even better ones also (even in basements) have mobile phone access. I know this may seem a bizarre choice, but it works well (remember, they have to be spotless!) and gives you a really calm place to pass some waiting time.

# An ongoing challenge

With more and more people taking the plunge into independent life, finding quiet corners to work will take increasing ingenuity. The other day, I was in a business club in London, and it was full at 10 o'clock with people – quite horrible. A two-minute walk away was a delightful (practically deserted) public library with a coffee shop attached and comfortable chairs! Where would you rather be? For many of us, life as an independent is going to mean a lot of time on the road. In doing this we can make it pleasant or just plain purgatory. Take a little time to discover what's available around where you need to meet people. You'll be surprised (and perhaps delighted) at what you'll find.

Travel can be the bane of our existence as independents or an opportunity to see and try out new things. Too many consultants seem to spend their days rushing around from place to place. They also always seem to be the ones who get delayed, or miss flight connections, or forget to book the hotel until it is overbooked. My advice is to try and slow down and think through what you want to do when you travel. Definitely go and see some more people if you can, stay over one more night and look for other opportunities. You'll never know if you don't try.

Certainly travel isn't as much fun as it used to be, but it is still a question of what you make it. And you can make it better – all you need to do is try.

# Key learning points

> Learn to travel light and learn to travel smart.

> Try and leave on days that are less busy.

> Negotiate hotel deals if you go back to locations on a regular basis; alternatively get your client's corporate rate.

> Better to buy cheap tickets and occasionally throw them away than to buy fully flexible at a huge premium.

> For 'on the road' expenses, develop a system to keep track of your costs and stick to it.

> Remember, today the workplace is everywhere. Learn to recognise and use those 'free' corners of airports, hotels and the rest.

# Chapter **11**

# Counting the cost (and the profit)

'Where there is income tax, the just man will pay more and the unjust less on the same amount of income.'

**Plato**

'Income tax has made more liars out of people than golf and fishing have.'

**Anon**

Possibly we should title this chapter 'The Responsible Independent Consultant', because whether we like it or not, we have to ensure that we pay our taxes and the rest. This has always been an area of doing business that I have preferred to leave to others who are a lot more qualified than me. I work on the basis that they are going to do it not only better but probably a lot cheaper at the end of the day than me trying – and getting wrong – some do-it-yourself approach.

My personal advice on this is to get the best advice you can afford, and, if it looks really cheap, that is what you will get – cheap advice. And, continuing with the philosophising, cheap advice is advice you cannot afford.

Taking my own advice, I am happy – not to say ecstatic – to turn the responsibility for much of the content in this chapter over to my own accountant, Peter Clegg, a senior partner of Westlake Clark in New Milton, Hampshire (www.westlakeclark.com). Not only have Peter and myself put this chapter together to try and iron out the basics of the tax and legal obligations you have as an independent consultant – and the different options open to you – we have gone a lot further than that.

What we have done – to give you the best possible up-to-date advice – is create a website (www.pearson-books.com/smarterconsulting) that has the very latest information on all the taxation, social security and other bits and pieces necessary to the independent's legal requirements. Here in the book we have confined ourselves to some basic information about what you need to have to make the legal parts of your business function properly. As of now, the website gives current details on UK requirements only.

If you have any questions on this section, be sure to e-mail Peter Clegg – he knows what he is doing: PeterC@westlakeclark.com.

> **1** **TIP** Don't forget! In all the basic examples and those on the website we use United Kingdom rules and regulations. Readers in other countries do need to consult local experts as tax liabilities and methods vary considerably.

## What do you need to make it?

This is a crucial question and one of the major reasons you have become an independent. You need to make enough to pay your taxes, outgoings and your household bills and possibly also for your partner/family. So, to make ends meet you need to look at your pricing model. What we have done is to give examples on our website.

# What kind of business suits you best?

Starting out to work fo yourself, there a few things you need to consider right away. Are you going to be a sole trader or limited company? How will you function as an independent? How do networks and partnerships work? And what is the right approach for you?

As an independent operating in the UK you have, basically, two real options. First, self-employed as a sole proprietor or sole trader. Second, you can run your business through a limited company. So what are the advantages, disadvantages and key features of each?

# Sole trader

## *Advantages*

> Confidentiality. Virtually no information is available about you in the public domain unless you want to put it there.

> Freedom of manoeuvre with very little regulation.

> Easy to operate.

> Easy to start and easy to finish.

> You pay tax each year on your profits as you earn them.

## *Disadvantages*

> Unlimited liability. If anything goes wrong, apart from any insurance cover that you may have (for public or employer's liability or indemnity insurance), you are totally and personally liable for any claims that are made against you.

> Tax planning is difficult as you pay tax on the profits as you earn them.

> Higher taxes than using a limited company currently.

# Limited company

## *Advantages*

> Easy to establish (you can buy or form a ready-made limited company for around £60 or less, if you shop around).

> Limited liability for the shareholders so most litigation should stop with the company, protecting the directors and shareholders and, in your case, you and your family.

> Tax planning can be easier.

> More tax efficient currently than the sole trader option.

## *Disadvantages*

> Some financial information needs to be on file in the public domain, principally at Companies House, where abbreviated annual accounts need to be filed, together with details of the company's directors, company secretary and shareholders.

> Higher administrative burden than being a sole trader, but, on balance not that much worse. For example, a limited company will need to operate a PAYE scheme for just you as a director.

By law in the UK, a limited company must have at least one shareholder, together with at least one director assisted by a company secretary. If you only have one director, then this person cannot also be the company secretary. Ask your spouse or partner to be your company secretary if this makes sense.

# Are there any other things you need to know?

Well, if you are starting off as an independent in a small way and want to test the water, then working as a sole trader is a cheap and inexpensive option, as you can, relatively painlessly, always convert your sole trading business to a limited company later on with very little tax downside. However, do not underestimate the importance of limited liability. Some of your clients, customers and suppliers may be vexatious litigants and using a limited company gives you a considerable element of protection (should it be necessary) plus a certain amount of kudos and status. To some clients you will always look more attractive as a limited company (however small) than as a sole trader.

*Note*: Compare the tax and accounting impact of these two options on the website.

# What about networks and partnerships?

Here again there are contrasts that need to be thought through, preferably before you get going.

## *Networks*

A network is defined as a group of like-minded individual sole traders or limited companies who work together on an informal basis by sharing work, contacts and resources. Crucially, however, all of the individuals within the network are likely to be 'independent', with each person running his or her own separate business. The network is in effect a mini trade association. So, in getting involved in a network there are some points to watch and worry about:

> Where does legal liability for any mistakes lie?

> Who is entitled to revenues and profits from a particular assignment?

> How do you share costs, including common costs such as websites, advertising and marketing?

> What happens when one of your network members runs off with your best client?

> How do you police your network? Can the bad behaviour of one member drag you all down?

All of these questions are hard to answer and differ widely, depending on the business you are in and how you perceive the network functioning on a day-to-day basis. However, simply put, they are best dealt with by all members of the network agreeing on a clear set of rules at the outset. Not having a clear-cut set of rules and an agreed way of working – and handling disputes – can create chaos further down the line. And disputes only take away from the productive energy of the group.

All too often enthusiasm for creating a business gets in the way of common sense. Starry-eyed entrepreneurs, excited by what appears to be boundless opportunity and even more boundless profits can be blind to down-to-earth reality. Please don't wait until the day things turn sour before you act – you'll regret it many times over. Just as closing stable doors after horses have bolted is pointless, so is trying to pick up the pieces of a business when once like-minded work colleagues fall out.

## Partnerships

Partnerships are a more formal way for people to work together. Basically, partnerships are governed in the following way.

> Partnership involves two or more individuals carrying on business together to generate profits, a legal definition that has survived, so far, unchanged from the Partnership Act 1890.

> Partners in a business have joint and several liability for all of the liabilities and obligations of the partnership. This means that if the partnership has unpaid bills and partner A cannot pay, then partner B is liable for all of the partnership's obligations.

> In tax law, a partnership is taxed in the same way as a sole trader would be, except that there are two or more individuals involved.

> A partnership agreement setting out the obligations and responsibilities of the partners to each other is a must. Otherwise the partnership is governed under the rules contained in the 1890 Partnership Act.

> Taking this a stage further, your partnership could trade as a limited company with each 'partner' being a director and shareholder in the limited company.

> As an alternative you could set up an LLP (a Limited Liability Partnership) which is, from a tax perspective, an ordinary partnership but which gives the individual partners limited liability, with the trade-off being the need to file financial information and accounts at Companies House.

# Getting in the professionals

What do accountants, solicitors, bookkeepers and bank managers do for you? Keep you out of trouble with the taxman for one thing! And how do you go about finding them?

Leaving aside the school of thought that 'people in suits can never help you', my advice is to always get professional help unless you are in the business yourself. So here is a brief guide to these backroom experts. But do remember that none of these individuals will make your business a success or a failure. They are just there to try and keep you on the straight and narrow, offering – perhaps – encouragement and support. Success or failure is entirely down to you.

> **2** **TIP** Don't try and get expert advice on the cheap. Get the best professional help you can reasonably afford. The best charge most. There's a reason for that, they are good at what they do. Cheap advice is just that, you could say that you'll pay for it one day!

## *Accountants*

Most accountants will have a professional qualification (e.g., being a member of one of the professional bodies). They should help you decide on the most appropriate structure for you, i.e. sole trader or limited company or partnership. Accountants are there to guide you through the taxation and administrative red tape of running your business so that you keep on the right side of the taxman, know what profit you can keep, pay your taxes on time, and steer clear of trouble.

How do you find a good accountant? The most reliable method is by word of mouth. Listen to recommendations and testimonials from friends and colleagues. Talk to two or three accountants to see what they can offer you and whether you get on with them on a personal basis. Ideally, you probably do not need an accountant who is working with an organisation that dwarfs yours in size – you need someone who is used to working with the problems that you will encounter. Find out what the prices will be for the various items of work that you need done. Identify how any extras or add-on services will be priced. Most accountants will charge you on an hourly basis and will give you a fairly good quotation for what your basic work needs will be. But, just like getting building work done at home, consider whether you will want any extras or whether you will want to vary the work specified, as this will invariably lead to extra cost. Talk through the time frame for providing information to your accountant and be clear as to where the responsibilities for providing information lie.

Finally, remember that your accountant should be enabling and empowering you to see your way through the regulatory and taxation framework and his advice could save you considerable amounts of tax, time and frustration. This is a critical choice to make, so put in the research and work to get the best you can.

## Legal support and solicitors

You will need a solicitor for those moments when you have a contractual dispute with a customer or supplier, are entering into a network or joint venture agreement or have issues to clarify on employment law, ranging from employment contracts all the way through to issues that might involve your being taken to an employment tribunal. High street solicitors tend to work mainly in the areas of conveyancing, matrimonial, wills and probate so you will want to be clear that the solicitor you choose can offer you support in these business-related areas. Generally, the bigger the legal practice, the more specialisation is available in the areas that you may need as an independent consultant. However, with this specialisation comes higher cost and the need for you to deal with a bigger legal firm in consequence.

Solicitors are also best chosen by recommendation and by selecting a firm that matches your current and future business needs and philosophy.

## Bookkeepers

If you do not want to run your own accounting software support package to keep your daily books and records up to date, you may want a bookkeeper to do this for you. Bookkeepers are much cheaper than accountants and will be able to offer you the one or two days per month or per quarter that you need to keep your records in order. They can cost anywhere between £15 to £40 per hour, depending on where you are located and depending on skill and quality. Again, word of mouth is quite helpful and your accountant should be able to point you in the right direction of a suitable bookkeeper. You must be prepared to pay the market rate to get the work done properly and efficiently.

## Bank managers

You will need, sooner rather than later, a separate bank account for your business receipts and payments. In any case, running the business as a limited company does, of necessity, require a bank account opened in the name of the limited company. Only if you are starting your life as an independent as a sole trader on a very small-scale basis can you really get along by continuing to use your own personal bank account.

# So what are the ins and outs of business banking?

> There will be bank charges for pay-ins and withdrawals, although most of the large banks will usually not make any charges for the first 12 months or longer.

> The days of an individual bank manager being a semi-permanent fixture within your chosen bank have long gone. Therefore building an ongoing rapport with the local manager is not very likely. Be prepared for the individual with whom you establish a relationship moving on sooner rather than later.

> Therefore, you need to choose your business bank based on the services it offers, such as free accounting packages, introductory 'free' banking periods and other services that you may need.

> You will almost certainly want a business charge card on your business bank account.

> If you want to borrow money for the business, you will find that the bank will want to put in place some form of security for this lending (such as a second mortgage on your home). They will also charge an arrangement fee and also charge you interest for the privilege. At this point it does pay to shop around for the best deals.

> Unsecured lending is usually only possible for relatively small amounts of borrowing, although you can explore the DTI-sponsored loan guarantee scheme.

> Secured lending will mean that if the business does collapse, you are still liable to the bank even if you are trading as a limited company.

> Do tell your bank what is happening with your business. Send them copies of your annual accounts, as this helps you to keep in touch and maintain a relationship, however tenuous.

> Do not go overdrawn without first discussing this with the bank – it makes it so much easier if you have been in touch beforehand and discussed the reasons why.

> In choosing a bank, you may want to use the same bank that provides your current personal checking account or mortgage or, maybe for diversity, to set up a relationship with a different banking provider. Shopping around is the obvious answer.

> Don't be afraid to change banks. Today, competition for customers is extreme and banks can make the switch for you without too much hassle. Terms and conditions vary widely, so be ready to move if it makes sense to do so.

## Contracts with clients

Do not work for free unless this is your choice, although pro bono work can be good for business reputation in the right place and under the right conditions. Make it clear up-front with your clients what your terms of business are, when you will invoice them and when you expect to get paid. Set this out in an exchange of letters (preferably) or e-mails with your supplier so that you are creating a binding understanding or contract between you and them. Make sure that your invoicing refers to the original contract between you and your client.

If you do not get paid, you may need to consider stopping work for your client. Try not to be fobbed off by excuses about cash-flow difficulties on their side. After all, if they are paying their own staff every month, why should they not pay you too? If you are having trouble getting paid, consider taking legal advice and if the contract you are setting up in the first place strikes you as complicated, take legal advice at this stage as well. This is where having a solicitor in place can really help you. Remember, as with all experts, it is better to have them on call when the need arises, rather than having a panic search to find one at the last minute.

## Working contracts with suppliers

Whatever you are buying in for your business, try to find out what this will cost and when you need to pay for it before you buy it. What payment terms do your suppliers require? Some items such as travel or life insurance have to be paid more or less instantly whilst other providers may give you at least 30 days' credit.

Try to agree similar contract terms or issues with your suppliers as you would with your own clients or customers as this can affect your cash-flow situation to a large degree.

## The taxman cometh

Just what are your legal obligations to the taxman? What can you claim for and how can you minimise your tax obligations?

To set the scene here, your obligations as to what you can claim for will differ slightly depending on whether you are a sole trader or a limited company. In the UK, the taxes you have to deal with are administered by the Inland Revenue and Her Majesty's Customs and Excise. The Inland Revenue has responsibility for national insurance and direct taxation, whilst HM C&E has responsibility for indirect taxation, principally – as far as you are concerned – Value Added Tax (VAT).

You will have three significant tax areas to keep under control: VAT; national insurance; and income tax and corporation tax.

## VAT (Value Added Tax)

This is a tax on goods and services, and particularly services that you will supply as an independent. It is a sales or turnover-based tax and will be levied on you regardless of your profitability. Your liability to be involved with VAT depends on whether your sales (commonly called turnover) exceeds £61,000 per year. Above this level of sales (or turnover) you have to register for VAT compulsorily. Below this limit you can register on a voluntary basis, which can be a good idea if your clients are VAT registered because they can recover the input VAT that you charge them, which means that financially you will be better off because you can reclaim input VAT on any supplies (subject to VAT) that you buy in.

The main rate of VAT is 17.5 per cent. Most supplies or services provided by independents will be subject to VAT at this standard rate, but there can be exceptions – such as for work done overseas, for example – for which the VAT rate could be 0 per cent. However, if in doubt, be prepared to charge VAT at 17.5 per cent and make sure (taking advice from your accountant or HM C&E in writing) that it is appropriate to charge any of your services at a rate other than 17.5 per cent. Remember that VAT is a self-assessing tax where you will be liable for any mistakes.

You normally pay over any VAT that you have charged on your sales revenue (less any input VAT on allowable purchases) on a quarterly basis and your quarterly VAT return needs to be filed with HM C&E within one month of each quarter end. If you miss this deadline for filing your VAT return and making payment, you will be penalised.

There are certain helpful schemes run by HM C&E to help independents, including:

> a flat-rate VAT scheme for businesses with a sales turnover of up to £150,000 per annum;

> an annual accounting scheme (as opposed to filing your VAT returns quarterly, although you will pay VAT on a [more or less] monthly basis, based on an estimate of your annual VAT due);

> reporting your VAT due based on sales revenues banked and supplies paid for (commonly called a 'cash accounting' basis), which means that you only have to pay over VAT after your clients have paid you, which is good for positive cash-flow planning.

Above all, with VAT, failing to register when you need to, because your sales turnover for the previous 12 months has exceeded £61,000 can cause you significant financial penalties and difficulties.

Something that you may find strange about VAT is that if (say) you are a sole trader, your VAT registration encompasses all business activities carried on by you personally, not just those that you carry out as an 'independent'. So if, for example, you carry out some freelance paid writing as a side-line activity and you are also an independent sole trader, then both activities are aggregated for the purposes of deciding whether you should register for VAT compulsorily, and also for working out your VAT each quarter, so that you would have to charge VAT on your freelance writing activities.

Finally, as with so many things in life, as VAT is a transaction-based tax, take advice before the transactions occur, so speak to your accountant or bookkeeper or the HM C&E helpline and get it right first time.

## National insurance

The contribution-based principles of the post-war Beveridge era are now well in the past, and national insurance – administered by the Inland Revenue – is now becoming, more and more, an earnings and payroll tax with increasingly little bearing on any state retirement pension you will receive. There are four classes of contributions:

Class 1 – paid by both employers and employees
Class 2 – payable by sole traders
Class 3 – voluntary contributions – which we will ignore
Class 4 – payable by sole traders
and
Class 1A – paid by employers only on taxable benefits provided to staff

Current details on these are available on the website.

## Income tax and corporation tax (and other direct taxes such as capital gains tax)

This area of taxation is administered by the Inland Revenue.

You will only come into contact with corporation tax if you trade through a limited company. The rate at which it is payable is usually – for an independent – around 19 per cent of the profit made by the company in each year. Any corporation tax is usually payable nine months after the end of the company's financial year end.

Whilst you may hear that the first £10,000 of profits are not subject to corporation tax, this will not be the case if you take dividends from your limited company – the corporation tax rate will then be much closer to 19 per cent. This is a good topic for you to discuss with your accountant or, if you have the time, to check out on the Inland Revenue's own website, (www.inlandrevenue.gov.uk). You can also find an example on our website.

## What can I claim for?

An overview of some of the common claimable and non-claimable costs is available on the website as well as for calculating and minimising your tax.

## Your legal obligations to the taxman

Each year, whether you are a sole trader or a limited company, you will have to file various sorts of tax returns with the Inland Revenue (and Companies House also if you operate as a limited company).

Most importantly, both sole traders and limited companies must submit their accounts annually to the Inland Revenue. You must also keep records of your revenues and costs, substantiated, as far as possible, by keeping receipts, copy invoices and bank statements. Also, these records should regularly be processed (particularly for a limited company which has an additional legal duty under the Companies Act 1985 to maintain regular accounting records).

## Getting a bank manager you can work with

Undoubtedly you can find a bank that you can work with, but finding a bank manager with whom you will always establish a good relationship may be difficult to start with. Bank managers, or business bankers as they may be known, are always anxious for promotion and advancement. Your must expect that your business relationship manager within your bank is going to move on.

To get the best out of your bank, you must work at maintaining the relationship. Provide information on a regular quarterly or six-monthly basis so that your bank manager knows what you are up to. The information you send can be profit and loss accounts and balance sheets together with any cash-flow forecasts that you might prepare.

Banks – just like you – do not like surprises. So if there is a difficult tax bill approaching that needs to be paid, talk to your bank manager in good time. Do not phone him the night before the cheque is about to clear or bounce! Recognise that your bank manager is not an independent and has to follow the rules. You must realise that he is still in that comfort zone of full-time employment with a salary cheque coming in every month!

## You need a loan like a hole in the head

Loans will cost you money, not only in interest charges but also in arrangement fees. Planning your cash-flow (see website for an example) should help you to ensure that your bank balance stays in credit.

Agreeing regular invoicing or billing patterns with your clients is important. You will find that working with clients who are larger than you – an inevitable consequence as an independent – means you are dealing with large organisations that will pay on credit terms of 30 or 60 days. Getting your invoicing done on time is important, and making sure that this matches the payment authorisation programmes of your suppliers as well.

So why do you need a loan? Probably it is only because you are not managing your own cash-flow positively, so think and plan ahead. Use your bookkeeper or accountant to help you develop planning strategies if you need to.

## Supplies, supplies, supplies

Here it pays, as always, to shop around. Use the Internet to seek out the best deals, but do heed the advice above and agree the terms of business with all your suppliers.

Don't forget though, that whilst it may be cheaper to buy some services and supplies online, from time to time you may need a more personal service and a local insurance broker or IT hardware engineer, used to dealing with unusual requests, may give you more immediate and more relevant service.

# Pension plans

This is certainly not a must-have early in your independent business, but you should review your needs carefully once you are established. You should, particularly, take detailed independent financial advice on the relevance and investment performance of any past pension entitlement that you may have built up with an employer prior to your independent life.

## *State retirement pension entitlement*

See the website for details.

# Hiring staff and subcontract help

Set out right from the start what the rules of engagement are, including how much you have to pay and when. Although it is cheaper – particularly from a tax perspective – to hire subcontract or freelance/self-employed assistance, it is the facts of the work that is actually done which determines whether it is employment or self-employment. If you are hiring staff on an employed basis, not only do you have to deal with employment legislation (including paid holidays, sick pay and other employment law issues) but you must operate the deduction of income tax and employee national insurance from any salary paid and you must also pay, on top, employer's national insurance. Therefore, if you are hiring staff, you need to budget for employer's national insurance contributions (see website for current details).

The Inland Revenue will expect you to get the employee/self-employed distinction correct, and if any self-employed consultants or freelancers are subsequently reclassified as employees by the Inland Revenue, then you and not your self-employed consultants or freelancers will be liable for any PAYE and NIC deductions that should have been made, together with penalties and interest.

## Accounting packages

There are some good entry-level accounting packages for the independent, such as:

> Sage instant

> Taz books

> Quicken

All of which can help to make your accounting life less stressful.

## Domain names and intellectual property rights

Whilst forming a limited company can help, in a small way, to protect your business name, you should also consider securing the domain name(s) for your business website.

You might also want to register a trade mark and other intellectual property rights if these are a significant asset to your business, and you would be susceptible to competitive infringement in these areas.

Finally do not underestimate the help you can obtain (both free of charge or subsidised) by using the DTI sponsored business link service (www.businesslink.org.uk). Attending their events can also be very helpful for networking opportunities.

## Working from home: claiming expenses

If you are working from home, then any extra household costs involved in running your office can be claimed for including:

> additional lighting and heating costs;

> office furniture;

> telephone, fax and Internet costs;

> additional insurance.

All of these costs can usually be claimed by means of a round-sum adjustment called 'use of home as office' which can range from £5 per week upwards depending on actual circumstance. Warning! Do not overclaim, as the Inland Revenue will scale back any unreasonable claims.

For sole traders – a reasonable (in the view of the Inland Revenue, not you), business-use related portion of your home mortgage interest can also be claimed.

Remember though, that if you are claiming a fixed proportion of your home costs against tax, then part of your home can become an asset for Capital Gains Tax purposes when you sell your home. So consider any claims that you make with care.

# Travel – the unromantic stuff you need to know

As an independent you are likely – certainly at the outset – to run your business from home. Therefore, most of your travel costs will be tax deductible, whether for train, car, plane or taxi. Do keep records and all the receipts as you will need these to substantiate any business expenses. Having said this, if you are working on a long-term project with one client from their offices, it is possible that your place of business for tax purposes may become your client's premises. At that point your home-to-work travel is effectively commuting and, therefore, the costs are not tax deductible any longer. For a more in-depth discussion of this topic, look at the Inland Revenue's own booklet which can be accessed at the following website addresses:

> http://www.inlandrevenue.gov.uk/guidance/480.pdf

> http://www.inlandrevenue.gov.uk/helpsheets/490.pdf

# Family and the independent consultant

Thinking of the tax issues, yes, you can pay your spouse or partner to work in your business. The golden rules are:

> The payments must actually be made by cheque or by cash.

> What you pay should be justified in terms of the duties carried out.

> What you pay should be in line with the national minimum wage.

> Make sure that what you pay is not excessive compared to your spouse's actual input and, by inference, tax driven. Otherwise any excess remuneration could then be reassessed on you if you are challenged by the Inland Revenue, leaving you liable to higher tax charges that you might not be anticipating.

Does your spouse or partner need a contract of employment? This is definitely a question for your solicitor! I am sure that the theoretical answer is 'yes' but the practical, real world answer might be 'no'.

You may wish (as an alternative to employment) your partner or spouse to be either a 'partner' in your sole trading business or a shareholder in your limited company. In this way, you could reduce the tax that you pay at higher rates by using up your spouse's or partner's unused basic tax rate band. The Inland Revenue are all too aware of this ploy and if your spouse or partner is not fully contributing to the business profits, then their profit share or dividends could be reassessed on you, negating any tax advantage. This planning strategy, together with the 'IR35' issue are the two most contentious independent tax issues in play currently in the UK.

Finally, can you pay your children? The strict answer is 'no', both for tax and employment law reasons. However, by the time your children have reached their early to mid teens, then paying modest sums for real business tasks performed, such as envelope stuffing and genuine administrative duties is acceptable, although strictly you will need permission from your metropolitan or county council up until the age of 16 to do so, otherwise you will be breaking the law.

# Cars and other vehicles

Unfortunately, as you will discover, this merits its own (not too) small section! To get one thing straight first, you will find that the tax system is pretty restrictive, focusing any tax deductions on the business use of your car, together with the capability of delivering some unpleasant surprises! See website for details.

# Dealing with deadlines

Finally, something that you are already used to, but with a difference. As either a sole trader or a limited company, you will have numerous extra deadlines to watch out for, apart from your normal work-related commitments. Missing any of them is likely to cost you money in terms of penalties, extra tax and interest on extra tax.

Here are some of the more important deadlines for both sole traders and limited companies:

# Both sole traders and limited companies

> **19 of each month**: PAYE/NIC payable on payroll deductions made in the previous month (although you will most likely be able to opt to pay your PAYE/NIC over quarterly as a 'small' employer).

> **31 January**: (a) File your personal tax return for the tax year ended on the previous 5 April and (b) Pay personal tax due (final, third or balancing payment for the previous tax year + first instalment for the current tax year).

> **19 April**: Interest runs on any PAYE/NIC due but, so far, unpaid for the tax year ended on 5 April.

> **19 May**: Form P35 (end of tax year payroll return) to be filed with the Inland Revenue. (Don't forget to give your staff their P60s too.)

> **30 June**: File child tax credit and working tax credit claim forms.

> **6 July**: Forms P11D to be filed reporting benefits in kind for staff (and directors, if a limited company). Don't forget to give your staff a copy of their form P11D too.

> **19 July**: Pay over any Class 1A NIC due on taxable benefits in kind.

> **31 July**: Pay personal tax due (second instalment for the tax year just finished).

> **Quarterly**: File your VAT returns and pay over any VAT due within one month of your VAT quarter end.

# Sole traders only

> **Within 3 months of starting as a sole trader**: Register to pay Class 2 NIC at the rate of £2.10 per week, by filing the form CWF1 with the Inland Revenue National Insurance Contribution Office.

# Limited companies

> **Within 9 months of the year end**: Pay any corporation tax due.

> **Within 10 months of the year end**: File (usually abbreviated) accounts with Companies House.

> **Within 12 months of the year end**: File the company's corporation tax return with the Inland Revenue.

Now you see why you need good advice from well-qualified professionals! Don't let this part of your operation slip. It might not be exciting, it might not bring you any money (quite the contrary), but you cannot afford to ignore it.

# Chapter **12**

# What's next for the independent consultant?

'Never work before breakfast. If you have to work before breakfast, eat your breakfast first.'

**Josh Billings**

'Mrs Thicknesse and I agreed that a business of his own was probably the only solution for him because he was obviously unemployable.'

**Peter De Vries**

Making predictions can be hazardous at the best of times. Trying to peer into the future of independent consulting is not easy. For most of us who have been around for years, we have seen the whole business change more than once. So the easy way out is to fall back on what I said earlier in the book: you have to accept that change takes place all the time and you have to adapt your business proposition to that.

Unfortunately, that isn't giving you much to go on. So here is a highly personalised view of what's coming in the next five years. Just don't complain to me if it doesn't work out this way.

## More competitors and more opportunity

I have little doubt that we are going to see an ever more crowded market as more and more people take up the challenges of working for themselves. Everywhere I look it seems that there are vast numbers of new entrants to the marketplace, all eager to prove that they have the skills to make it on their own.

Quite frankly, I don't see this as a bad thing. The main reason for my optimism is that there is an increasing amount of business out there for the taking. From my viewpoint, many mainstream businesses in both the public and private sector are reluctant to return to the high levels of full-time staff they once employed. Most of them it seems would rather outsource specialised work to external suppliers. Equally, as more and more work becomes intensely specialised, companies feel that they get a better deal hiring talent when they need it for short-term assignments than keeping it permanently on the books.

This is borne out by the massive increase in the temporary, or interim, workforce in both Europe and the US; a trend that shows no signs of slowing down. For years, employment experts have predicted real changes in how people get jobs and build careers and this looks like finally coming to fruition. This opens many new doors of opportunity for the independent consultant, which we are only just beginning to see and capitalise on.

In the course of putting this book together, I have spoken to scores of independent consultants who have basically outsourced themselves from their former workplaces and taken a tiny piece of the business with them. Well it may be tiny for the mega corporation, but not for the individual. In some cases these border on the farcical.

For example, a publisher was fired after 15 years in a job because she was the longest serving employee, and therefore (corporate logic decreed) the most expensive. Having terminated her – with full redundancy payments, I hasten to add – they then turned around and asked her if she could, 'please, please, please' act as the editorial consultant on the two publications she used to work on as they had no one with the expertise to do them. It gets worse (or, in her case, better). She called me and together we worked out the time it would take her, and the rate she should charge per day. Last year she made 150 per cent of her previous annual salary from the comfort of her own home. They – still in a fix and faced with a total hiring freeze – are signing her up again.

Stories like this abound and are going to increase. When you talk to big corporations these days, you quickly realise that they don't actually like people very much. Why? Well, in truth, people are messy and prone to break down and cry and have stress-related problems. So, if you can banish them from your offices (saving on office space too), and still get them to do the work, so much the better.

We are all seeing the reality of the 'virtual' office, and that is the playground of the independent consultant. Whether you are editing books, coaching people, handling legal claims, doing the accounts or creating sales campaigns, more and more companies would rather have you at a distance than on their premises. The great thing is that this is a truly win-win situation. You can get paid well (certainly as well as when you were employed full-time) and the employers save money by not having to worry about social security, pensions, healthcare and those pesky office costs.

As I said earlier, my local neighbourhood – 70 miles from London's metropolis – is now home to the twenty-first-century equivalents of the artisan class. All of them are refugees – happy, grateful, smiling refugees – I should add, from the hateful corporate commute. They write, they sell, they organise, they are the New Age independent and they are here to stay.

One of my new neighbours markets exotic resort locations (all online) in faraway lands. Another consults to care homes for the elderly. A third is a lawyer specialising in trade-mark disputes. They all have the need to travel (but not every day) and they all have the ability to work from a semi-rural location, where a great infrastructure means they can get to most places pretty fast. Ten years ago, they may have struggled to do this. Today it is second nature and none of them would swap this kind of life for that of an employee ever again. Sure, sometimes you won't make as much money, but then you don't spend as much either and your quality of life is so much higher.

Not all would-be independent consultants will want to do that. Many will stay in the cities, content not to have that commute each morning and evening – using that time to work instead of putting up with the commuter crush. All I know is that we will see an increasing number of the best and the brightest taking this option and baling out of mainstream employment.

# Technology takes over

Whether we like it or not, technology will drive how, where, why and when you work, and possibly what you work at too. For most independent consultants – especially those working from their homes – technology-related costs will be the single most expensive budget item (and you will need to be smart and budget upgrades and the like into your operating plan). Having said that, technology costs tend to come down, so we are not talking about the huge investments of the past.

Breakthrough technologies allied to breakthrough applications of those same technologies will govern a lot of what the independent consultant does next and the types of opportunity that open up. We can already work fairly efficiently at a distance; tomorrow those distances will be even greater. Why sit 50 miles from your client in some rainy, grey suburb in Northern Europe, when you can do your work from a sun-kissed veranda overlooking the Mediterranean? I already know people doing this, flying in to see their clients once a month or so.

This, I consider, will be the next big trend for many of us. Apart from the odd desk-bound manager who gets insanely jealous (and, yes, there are some like that!), most intelligent corporate types look to the quality of the work rather than where you do it from. But before you haul out the bucket, spade and beach towel, a word of caution. If you do decide to move, please pick a place where you can get back to your clients quickly and reliably. Quality of work counts, but so does availability and being seen on a regular basis.

Here's a cautionary tale. An IT consultant bailed out and went to live in the Outer Hebrides. His work arrived online. For a year he was happy, going back to see his former work colleagues every three months. It looked idyllic. It looked too good to be true. And, as I have said throughout this book, if a thing looks too good to be true, it probably is.

A year after he started work, I interviewed him for an article I was writing. I asked him, 'Apart from the local way of life, what is the best thing about working at a distance from your company?' Without hesitation, he replied, 'office politics'. Six months later, my interviewee had lost his job. Reason? Office politics. Basically, he hadn't been around to defend his position when the first round of job cuts came along. His work 'colleagues', probably mildly jealous anyway, had seen to it that he was the first to go. And while being kicked out is not a nice experience in a city, it is a waking nightmare in a remote location. My advice here is that if you do make that kind of jump, know where the parachute can be found and how to pull the rip-cord, you may well need it. Just like we talked about priming the pump, part of any adventure like working in a very remote location is starting out – day one – seeking other options if things do turn sour.

The lesson here is that, yes, technology can free us, but it needs to be managed. Sadly, unless you are a one-of-a-kind genius, being away from the action makes you vulnerable. This isn't technology at work, it's human nature.

All the same, the ability of virtually all of us to invest in what is now relatively cheap technology does make setting up on our own a workable proposition. These days £1,000 (€1,500) will get us access to the kind of technology our corporate brethren have access too as well. But HOW you use it will continue to drive the role of the independent.

As I have already said in previous chapters, new breakthroughs like multi-location video conferencing, will change forever how we meet. Some consultants will develop this as a core skill, giving themselves a huge advantage over those who don't do well 'on camera'.

## Consulting in the virtual world

Then, of course, there is the ultimate consultant destination – the virtual world. Already in virtual worlds like Second Life, consultants are setting themselves up in business and making real money. Major corporations are involved and have already hired – and outsourced – people who can live and work in these worlds. Expect this to be a massive growth area as people develop both products and services and – just like consultants in the real world – offer their expertise online.

## Staying up to date

And this is the other thing. We will need to stay up to date all the time. That old-fashioned idea that we learn (how to be an accountant or a psychologist for example) and then spend the next 30 odd years practising is obsolete. Everyone who expects to survive as an independent will have to keep on learning. And as those technologies arrive, we will have to not only learn how to use them but how to BEST use them for ourselves and to improve our offering to our customers.

All of us are so much more productive today than even five years ago. We don't need much back-up support. We can turn out reports and proposals in hours rather than days. We can book our own travel, order our supplies online. Everything, it seems, is possible from our own desks.

Except one thing, getting that face-time with the client. And even harder, getting to see the next business prospect.

This is going to be THE big issue for many would be go-it-aloners. I see it – witness it – myself every day. All those hard-pressed executives (who we need business from) just don't have the time to meet up with you. Most of them don't have the time to meet up with their own employees either, if that makes you feel any better. Don't expect this to improve any time soon. As independent consultants we are just going to have to work out ever more cunning ways to get onto these people's radar screens. The irony is that we have the technology to do that and – even worse – they want to buy what we have to offer, but the time gremlins make it almost impossible to sit down and have any kind of creative, meaningful conversation.

## MORE ON INTELLECTUAL PROPERTY (IP)

We live in a wonderful 24/7 world, where access to information is practically universal. While this can be great for prospecting for business, researching the market and so on, it does give rise to some concerns. For many independent consultants our ideas, our systems and methods are the only currency we possess. Lose those and we are out of business. For that reason – in this increasingly open society – we are more and more vulnerable to people and organisations who seek out and steal the work, ideas and concepts of others. Guard against this as best you can. As I have pointed out throughout this book, never give too much away – you are opening yourself up to be pirated. Make sure that you keep details of your services (especially on websites) to a minimum. Put a copyright symbol on any published material and any PowerPoint slides you use. If you get into relationships with others, have an exchange of letters about who owns the right to what. Is it tedious? Yes, it often is. But if you don't do it you may live to regret it. Your ideas are your own – guard them with your life. Because that is what they are – your life!

# Shorter relationships

At the risk of sounding pessimistic, I think that we are entering an age where long-term consultant–client relationships will practically cease to exist. Of course there will always be the exceptions (the independent financial consultant who does the annual tax return for a local client for 20 years), but for most of us, our relationships will be short and extremely intensive. And we had better be able to adapt our work style to this emerging model.

I believe that we are headed for a period of major disruption. Following years of recession and caution, we are now seeing an upsurge. This may augur well for the independent consultant in terms of more work, but it also means that those that give us the work are going to be a lot more unstable and unavailable. Truth is that inside public and private organisations there is an increasing 'churn' of executives as they begin to switch jobs. This is happening both internally (being moved to another position) and externally (finding a new job in a new firm).

## Selling to the organisation

To add to this, are two other indicators:

1 Executives are increasingly busy, and have less and less time.
2 Merger and acquisition activity is on the rise.

What all this does is create an interesting dilemma for the independent consultant, which we need to find creative ways to solve. If our 'targets' spend less and less time in one position, we have to give up on the idea of selling to the individual one way or another and be able to sell to the organisation. This means finding ways to maintain our place inside the client's business long after the person who originally gave us the work has gone.

I do believe that the concept of selling to a business and not to an individual is going to be a paramount skill in the coming years. That means being able to attract the attention and curiosity of people you don't know – have never met. This is where all that work on your network, building a reputation, creating research and so on will help enormously.

We may well have to move to a model similar to the way that the Chinese do business. You don't knock on a Chinese door and ask for business. Instead you create a need for them to come to you. If we stop and consider, most of us know that what we have to offer IS needed by big business (and not so big business too). If we can tickle their taste buds and get them to want to know more, then we have the makings of a sell on our hands.

We are all going to have to get better at the marketing aspects and less of the straight sell. Yes, it will take longer (plan for that), but it will also offer those of us who succeed great business opportunities. How do we make that happen? Well look back at Chapters 7 and 8 and consider what you can become and how you can best present yourself and your unique offering.

So our networks will need to expand and our business development activity be cranked up just to get the business. I predict shorter relationships with individuals, which is why you need to get into the business not the person. True, some of them may well remember you in their new job, but will it offer the right opportunities? Yes, they may recommend you to the incoming manager, but will he or she have their own contacts? You are better off selling to the business and not to the manager in charge. You'll last a lot longer.

Even with a wily plan to hook your prey by stealth and piquing their curiosity, expect tough times ahead and be ready to renew clients at an ever faster pace. All those tricks for never making cold calls described earlier in the book will become not just necessary but the only way to 'sell'.

## The arrival of the portfolio consultant

Not only will our clients change, there will also be new types of consultants out there. While some purists might not want to label them out-and-out consultants, my view is that they are and will have a major impact on the overall business in the years to come. I call them the portfolio consultant. These are bright, intelligent people who have decided that they want to work, but intend to use a variety of skills and a variety of different options to provide them with a living.

The first ones I have come across are professionals who took time off for children and now want to work without any commuting hassles or strict time commitments. While they may be a small group at present, I predict that this will become a major growth area in the next few years.

Here's an example. A former partner in a highly successful translation business took four years off to see her son through his pre-school years. Now that he is headed for school, she wants to work at something interesting, but also be able to take time off when she needs it at holidays and so forth (returning to a 9 to 5 job would mean the possibility of just three weeks off each year, certainly at the beginning). Using her excellent former client and translator/editor network, she has now set herself up in the following way using her hard-earned skills:

> **Activity 1: Freelance editorial consultant**. Currently working with two publishers to handle the pre and post publication editorial process on specialised books. Organises copy-checkers, proof readers, checks texts and recommends changes. Occasional visits to authors and the publishers' offices.

> **Activity 2: Freelance translator/reviewer**. Works with agencies in London, Brussels and Paris revising and reshaping texts. This is fast turnaround activity, but can be carried out anywhere there is a 'space' to download texts. She can do this basically 24/7, even on vacation if required.

> **Activity 3: Freelance research consultant** for a leading executive search firm. Following the recession, when all the freelance researchers were forced to find other work, there is a huge shortage of people. Works on a project-by-project basis that suits her time-scale.

> **Activity 4: Bric-a-brac hunter!** Her frequent car trips from the UK to Europe are usually underwritten by shipping over 'desirable', cute, bucolic, English 'junk', that Brussels Eurocrats pay top Euro for.

While never a threat to the top-end independent consultant, people like this are joining the ranks on a daily basis. They are smart, instinctively know how to multi-task and are full of enthusiasm. That's a powerful combination!

Recently, I met another independent consultant in the same sort of situation. Her portfolio is different, but again plays to her skills in her old career – teaching. She has established an intensive English language school for primarily French-speaking children (she is French herself) at her rambling home on the south coast of England. She takes four children at a time and offers a complete package of teaching and leisure activities. At the same time (or when the school isn't working) she translates texts and freelances as a market researcher, using her knowledge of teaching with children with learning difficulties and autism.

Again it is a portfolio of activity, but they all complement each other.

---

# Finally, the independent's secret

No book about this noble profession would be complete without a confession (one that I hope other independents will forgive me for). You can do a lot better than most people – on the outside – think. I mean that in terms of making a decent, worthwhile living. While I am not suggesting that everyone is going to have the take-home pay of a senior vice president of a *Fortune 500* corporation, you can make a very comfortable living. And you can do that, while making your own decisions and doing business on your own terms. Well, most of the time at least.

I recall only too well a younger colleague of mine who quit his job in a large corporation and set up in business on his own. I fed him some work in his early months to help him get started and he quickly turned out to be a great business developer as well. Sure he worked hard, but he was amazed to discover that after six months he had made a lot more money than he ever had as an employee. Moreover, he had enjoyed himself too! A few of my colleagues and I took him out to lunch to celebrate his discovery that working for yourself could be a lot more lucrative than he had supposed. We left him with the stern and strict admonition, 'Don't tell anybody.'

Certainly there are times when things go wrong – they do in the big, nasty corporate world as well. But at the end of the day, independent consulting is a lot more fun and something you can do for ever as long as your brain is working.

Looking back over 20 plus years as an independent, I have had a lot of fun, learned a lot, and hopefully given good advice and counsel to my clients. But the great thing is that I am not looking at a date on a calendar when I will have to retire. I can do this as long as I want. I may not do quite as much, but it is a better prospect than a sudden end to one's career at 60 or 65. It is even better than being told when you are 55 that you are over the hill and not worth being employed.

My advice – what this book is for – is to give it a go. It doesn't matter how old you are, anyone can do it – if they want to. You'll never know what it's like until you try. And then, be a pal, DON'T TELL ANYBODY!

## Key learning points

> There will be more competitors but also more opportunity as companies seek to outsource and contract out non-critical work.

> Technology will rule. Like it or not, we will just have to use it to the best of our abilities.

> We are headed for an era of shorter relationships with clients, brought about by an ever-changing working world. So expect to spend more time seeking and winning business.

> Guard your intellectual property. It is your business – literally!

> The portfolio consultant and multi-tasking will become the norm, taking on different types of business.

> Finally, the 'secret'. When you discover it's true, don't tell – EVER!!

# Appendix

Next time you need an agreement, use this one. It has stood the test of time and can cover just about any eventuality. How do I know that? I've used it for 10 years and it was put together by some very expensive legal experts. For ease of use, you can download it on the website www.pearson-books.com/smarterconsulting

## SAMPLE CONSULTANCY AGREEMENT

**BETWEEN:**   **Name here** (Hereinafter referred as the Company)

**AND:**   **Name here** (Hereinafter referred to as the Consultant)

**WHEREAS**:

Whereas the Company wishes to obtain advisory and consulting services from the Consultant as its independent external consultant for business development and the Consultant agrees to assist the Company with such services as an independent external consultant under the terms and the conditions set forth in this Agreement.

### NOW THEREFORE IT HAS BEEN AGREED AS FOLLOWS:

### Article 1  Subject

1. The Company hereby appoints the Consultant as its external consultant and the Consultant hereby agrees to provide independent advisory and consulting services to the Company in the field of (to be completed).
2. The tasks of the Consultant shall consist in the development of new clients (approved in advance by the Company) in the aforestated field including discussion of terms and conditions with actual or potential clients but with the exception of the signing of any contractual undertaking in that respect, unless specifically authorised by the Company.
3. The Consultant shall carry out its services as specified in the present Consultancy Agreement.

### Article 2  Duration and termination

1. This contract (hereafter the Agreement) shall enter into force for an indefinite duration on (to be completed).

2. The present Agreement may be terminated by each party with one (1) month advance written notice per commenced period of seniority of one (1) year and without exceeding in total six (6) months sent by registered mail, which takes effect the third working day following the date of mailing. The end of the notice coinciding with the end of the calendar month.

3. In the event that the serious misconduct or serious fault is of such a nature that it renders impossible the definitive continuation of any professional relationship, the aggrieved party shall have the right to terminate the Consulting Agreement at once, without notice or indemnity, by sending a registered letter to the other party in which the termination is effected and by sending, also by registered mail, within seven (7) days thereof the facts or reason justifying such termination for cause.

4. The Agreement shall automatically terminate in case of death or disability of the Consultant without notice or indemnity.

### Article 3  Conditions of performance of services

1. The Consultant shall perform the services in a completely independent manner and under its sole responsibility. The Consultant cannot commit or otherwise bind the Company unless specifically authorised by the Company. The services provided under this contract shall be rendered by the Consultant, via its President or via any other person designated by the Consultant subject to the prior express approval of the Company.

2. The Consultant shall perform the services conscientiously and shall devote his best efforts and abilities thereto, at such time during the term thereof, in such manner as the Company and the Consultant shall mutually agree.

3. The Consultant shall perform his activities under the present Agreement on an entirely independent basis and will never act or consider himself as an employee or agent of the Company. This agreement shall not constitute a partnership between the parties hereto.

   Without prejudice to its general obligation of proper performance of the services, the Consultant shall be able, with complete freedom and independence, to organise its activities and shall only have to render account of the specific duties or services accomplished under the present Agreement, but shall not be required to account for his working methods. The Company shall never exert over the Consultant any part of authority, which an employer is normally vested with.

The Consultant is solely responsible for the payment of the social security contributions and tax obligations, including VAT, with respect to the fees paid under the present Agreement.

4. This Consultancy Agreement is non-exclusive. The Company is free to consult other experts in the Consultant's field of specialisation and the Consultant retains the right to provide similar services to other parties, unless those parties carry on any activities in competition with the activities of the Company.

### Article 4  Copyright/confidentiality

1. The Consultant transfers to the Company, the future copyright in or on any and all written documents prepared by the Consultant for the Company or upon the Company's request within the framework of this Agreement.

2. The Consultant acknowledges that during the course of the consulting activities within the framework of this Agreement confidential information regarding the Company may be exchanged between the contracting parties. The Consultant shall keep secret and confidential all such information during the course of the Agreement and after the termination of this Agreement. The Consultant shall not use such information other than for this Agreement.

   Such information includes but is not limited to:

   ➤ All drawings, formulae, specifications, books, software, instruction manuals, daily reports, minutes of meetings, journals and accounts, business and trade secrets, oral or written data, whether concerning the existing or future business, methods, processes, techniques or equipment of the Company, its parent Company, subsidiaries or branch offices;

   ➤ The identity of the client's Company, its parent company, subsidiaries or branch offices and any other information relating to such clients.

3. Any violation of the secrecy obligation during the course of the present Agreement may be considered by the Company as a cause justifying immediate termination of the present Agreement, without notice and without prejudice to the right of the Company to claim damages.

4. Upon termination of this Agreement or upon the Company's request, the Consultant shall return to the Company all documents of whatever nature, notes, reports, letters and faxes relating to the Company and which he has received for the execution of the present Agreement.

### Article 5 *Non-competition and unfair competition*

The Consultant will refrain from actively soliciting the clients for which he has actively worked during the last two (2) years under this Agreement for a period of one (1) year after termination of this Agreement, in areas associated with this Agreement.

### Article 6 *Compensation*

1. [The time period and percentage amounts can be modified as required] In the event that the Consultant brings in an assignment, the Company shall pay (after receiving payment from the client) a fee equal to xx% (xx per cent) in the first year, xx% (xx per cent) in the second year and xx% (xx per cent) in the third year of the monthly net sum billed to the clients brought by the Consultant, during a period of three (3) years following the first invoice sent to the client by the Company. The consultant shall be paid in (state currency).

   When the Consultant is working for the Company, on their request, on projects gained by the Company, the Company shall pay to the Consultant a fixed daily fee in (state currency plus VAT). This fee shall be determined in advance by the Company and paid against submission of a monthly invoice.

2. The Consultant has the right to ask to see documents relating to the amounts billed to the clients and the payments made by clients in order to verify the amount due to him.

3. In addition to the compensation fixed in the first paragraph of this article, subject to the remittance of invoices, notes or any mutually acceptable evidence, the Company shall also reimburse expenses, subject to prior approval by the Company.

   In case there exists already contacts with the client and the Company, no fees will be due to the Consultant, unless the development of that relationship with the client is approved in advance in writing by the Company.

4. Upon termination of this Agreement, for whatever reason, the Consultant shall be entitled to receive the contractual compensation for all business brought until the date of actual termination of the agreement.

   Except in case of termination for cause, the Consultant shall also be entitled to the contractual compensation for any business brought by him or attributable to him, which the Company can invoice to such clients within six (6) months following the date of actual termination of the Agreement.

### Article 7  Assignment

No party to this Agreement may assign or delegate any of its/his rights, duties, powers or responsibilities thereunder without prior consent of the other party, given in writing.

### Article 8  Notice

All notices to be given under this Agreement, except in case of termination, shall be made by registered mail or by courier to the address of each party.

### Article 9  Severance and public restrictions

If any provision of this Agreement is declared void or unenforceable by any judicial or administrative authority, this shall not nullify the remaining provisions of this Agreement, provided that the cancellation of such provision does not substantially alter the economic interest of either party in the continued performance of this Agreement.

### Article 10  Governing law and jurisdiction

This Agreement is governed and interpreted in accordance with the laws of (give country or state). Any dispute arising in connection with this Agreement and which cannot be settled on an amicable basis shall be submitted to the exclusive jurisdiction of the courts of such a state.

### Article 11  Prior agreements

This Agreement constitutes the entire agreement between the parties relative to the matters referred to herein and supersedes any other agreement, whether oral or writing, which may have existed between the Company and the Consultant.

Any modification or amendments of this Agreement shall be in writing and shall become effective if and when signed by both parties.

Executed in two (2) original copies, each party acknowledging having receipt of one original copy,


By:_____

_____
Date


By : _____

_____
Date

# Index